We Have Not Vanished

WE HAVE NOT VANISHED

EASTERN INDIANS OF
THE UNITED STATES

Alfred Tamarin

Illustrated with Photographs

FOLLETT PUBLISHING COMPANY, CHICAGO

PHOTO CREDITS

Abby Aldrich Rockefeller Folk Art Collection, Williamsburg, Va., 91 top; Bureau of Indian Affairs, Department of the Interior, 120, 125, 126; Courtesy Chief Harold Tantaquidgeon, Uncasville, Connecticut, 55; Courtesy Howard Skye, Brantford, Ontario, 73; Florida News Bureau, 141, 143, 145, 146, 147, 149; Indian Arts and Crafts Board, Department of the Interior, 123, 127; Maine State Highway Commission, 30; Rhode Island Development Council, 47; Smithsonian Institution, National Anthropological Archives (negative numbers), 15 (56,930), 75 (43,792-A), 87 (56,930), 121 (44,384); Smithsonian Institution, National Anthropological Archives, Bureau of American Ethnology, 19 (3815(8)), 65 (963-a-5 (R)), 83 (4329), 102 (872-B), 103 bottom (873-B), 131 (3815 (14)), 134 (1169-L-3), 135 (1129-a); Smithsonian Institution, National Anthropological Archives, Boehmer Collection, 21 (45,217-K); Smithsonian Institution, National Portrait Gallery, 103 top (066239); United States Army Corps of Engineers, Pittsburgh District, 91 bottom; All others by the author, 17, 27, 29, 35, 38, 49 both, 59, 61, 67, 77, 95, 104, 105, 106, 108, 109, 118

Text copyright © 1974 by Alfred Tamarin. Illustrations copyright © 1974 by Follett Publishing Company, a division of Follett Corporation. All rights reserved. No portion of this book may be reproduced in any form without written permission from the publisher. Manufactured in the United States of America.

ISBN 0-695-40332-X   Titan Binding
ISBN 0-695-80332-8   Trade Binding

Library of Congress Catalog Card Number: 73-90052

First Printing

CONTENTS

ACKNOWLEDGMENTS

Deep appreciation is extended to the following Indian chiefs, leaders, historians, and friends who reviewed the indicated sections, arranged as they appear in the book:

Susan M. Stevens, Mt. Vernon, Maine—*Passamaquoddy*
Theodore N. Mitchell, Old Town, Maine—*Penobscot*
Russell H. Gardner, Whitman, Massachusetts—*Wampanoag*
Zarah Ciscoe Brough, Grafton, Massachusetts—*Nipmuc*
Rev. Harold Mars, Wakefield, Rhode Island—*Narragansett*
Gladys Tantaquidgeon, Uncasville, Connecticut—*Mohegan*
Chief Irving Powless, Jr., Nedrow, New York—*Onondaga*
Marlene Johnson, Steamburg, New York—*Seneca*
Chief Arnold Hewitt, Lewiston, New York—*Tuscarora*
James "Lone Bear" Reney, New York, New York—*Lenni Lenape*
John Witthoft, Philadelphia, Pennsylvania—*Pooles*
Kenneth S. Clark, Millsboro, Delaware—*Nanticoke*
Chief Curtis L. Custalow, Lester Manor, Virginia—*Mattaponi*
Chief O. Oliver "Lone Eagle" Adkins, Providence Forge, Virginia —*Chickahominy*
Lew Barton, Pembroke, North Carolina—*Lumbee*
Chief W. R. "Talking Eagle" Richardson, Hollister, North Carolina —*Haliwa*
Gwen Owle, Cherokee, North Carolina—*Cherokee*
Joe Dan Osceola, Hollywood, Florida—*Seminole*

In addition to the above Indian leaders who helped the author by reviewing the material about their tribes, thanks are due the following for advice, suggestions, and general assistance:

Maine and Canada: Governor John Stevens of the Passamaquoddy, and Maine Commissioner of Indian Affairs; Barry Nicholas; Dennis Nicholas; Willard Walker, Wesleyan University; Dean Snow, State University, Albany; Meredith Ring, Maine Indian Education Society, Calais; Jacob Ezra Thomas, Mohawk Institute, Brantford, Ontario.

Massachusetts: Gale Huntington; Mrs. D. Osborn Bettencourt; Gertrude H. Aiken; Emma O. Mills.

Rhode Island: Ethel Boissevain, Lehman College, New York;

Everett "Tall Oak" Weeden; Princess Redwing; Leonard J. Panaggio, Rhode Island Development Council; Alexander Ricciardelli, Brown University; Barbara Hail, Haffenreffer Museum.
Connecticut: Rose Harrison, Connecticut State Library.
New York: John R. Hathorn, Coordinator, Indian Affairs, Albany; Louis Jones, Milo V. Stewart, T. R. Jones, and David Robinson, New York State Historical Society, Cooperstown; Dr. Omar Ghobashy; Ray Fadden, Six Nations Museum; Arleigh Hill, Museum of Science, Rochester.
Pennsylvania: William A. Hunter, Chief, Division of History, Pennsylvania Historical and Museum Commission.
Delaware: C. A. Weslager; Department of Community Affairs, Dover.
Maryland: William B. Marye, Maryland Historical Society; Herbert R. Locklear.
Virginia: Ben C. McCarey; Milton C. Russell and Ethel M. Slonaker, Virginia State Library.
North Carolina: Theodore Krenzke, Cherokee Agency, Bureau of Indian Affairs; William S. Pollitzer, University of North Carolina School of Medicine; Stephen Richmond, Department of the Interior; Judith R. Sutton, State Library; Memory F. Mitchell, Department of Archives and History.
Florida: Buford Morrison, Miccosukee Agency, Bureau of Indian Affairs: Eugene Barrett, Seminole Agency, Bureau of Indian Affairs; Mary Lou Norwood, Florida News Bureau.
General: Mary Ellen Ayres, Bureau of Indian Affairs; Henry H. Smith, Bureau of the Census; Myles Libhardt, Department of the Interior, Washington, D.C.; Jeannette Henry, American Indian Historical Society, San Francisco.

FOREWORD

I first met the author and his wife in New York City after he had contacted one of my friends. He told me that he was going to write a book about the Native Americans on the East Coast. I liked his idea of the book, which was to inform readers that Native Americans still exist in the East. I had read in some books that we did not exist anymore. This had always troubled me since I knew of no way to inform people that we are still around and that we had not been extinguished. The object of this book was to say "Hello. Here we are. We are fine."

Since our first meeting, the author and I have met to discuss the book and its contents, and from time to time I would hear from him about his progress.

He was doing something that many writers fail to do. He was meeting the people he was writing about and asking them "What do you want said about your people?" and "What do you want changed from the usual writing?" And he was allowing the people to see what he had written before it was published.

Many misconceptions about the Native Americans have been passed along through the years. This book offers an opportunity to have some of these stereotypes dispelled. It is very important to us that people realize we still exist and are still carrying out the duties that were handed down to us by our ancestors.

The author has read many of the books about the Native Americans, and he realized that something was missing from these books. After discussing his book, I pointed out that most books referred to us in the past tense. There was a need to update this information and inform people that the Native Americans are still here. There was also a need to tell where and how they live today as compared to yesterday.

I told the author that I would be willing to help him on the chapters about my people, but I could not speak for the rest of the Indian nations and communities.

This book does not cover the details of our existence, our social or religious life, but instead allows the reader to know where the Indian communities are throughout the East Coast. Some of our people are in the cities, and some are still living on the original lands that our people occupied before the coming of the white man.

Books are a vehicle by which we may meet many people of many countries. Come with us and meet the Native Americans who are still a part of this country, just as they were when your ancestors first came to the shores of what is now called America.

IRVING POWLESS, JR.
Chief, Onondaga Nation

dedicated to all Native Americans in the Eastern United States

PREFACE

The New Mexican sun shines hot and bright on the plaza in Santa Fe. Three historic population strains rub shoulders with casual disinterest. The descendants of northern European settlers still bustle despite the dry heat. The grandchildren of Spain, whose forefathers had arrived in the southwestern United States before the Pilgrims landed, speak with a lilt in their voices. And silently passing back and forth are the Indians, who were first and still remain, no matter how the world has changed around them.

Watching the straight-backed, solemn-faced Navajo and Pueblo Indians set some insistent questions racing through my mind. My own earliest years were spent near the Dutch, who came exploring my own homeland in the Hudson River Valley, the meeting grounds of four divergent peoples: the English, the Iroquois, the Algonquians. What had become of the Indian people of the Atlantic seaboard states? Where were the descendants of the native people who helped the first European colonists survive in a new world?

Official maps of Indian communities from government offices in Washington, D.C., showed empty spaces along the Atlantic coast. Had the Indians really vanished, as so many books said? To find the answer re-

quired long hours of research and weeks of travel—
from the top of Maine to the foot of Florida. It meant
visiting with historians, librarians, university professors,
newspapermen, photographers, state officials, and key
representatives of the Bureau of Indian Affairs, both
in Washington and in the field. But most important, it
involved fascinating hours with the Indian peoples
themselves, their chiefs, their community leaders,
their teachers, their wives, husbands, and children.
Sometimes the venerable chiefs listened patiently,
probably as they had on hundreds of occasions before.
Sometimes a younger, more energetic voice had a
new tone. We'll talk; you listen. And I did with eager
attention.

There is still much to be learned about our Indian
neighbors in the East. Colonial history moved with
great speed, particularly around the eastern tribes
who made no effort to preserve their history in written
records. Research of all kinds is being undertaken—
from blood typing to folk history. Languages are being
revived and written alphabets devised for them. But
there is much more social history to be explored and
preserved. And younger Indian scholars and writers
may be the ones to undertake the challenge.

Personally I consider myself indebted to many of
my Indian neighbors for advice and hospitality. Many
supplied me with information and photographs. Some,
whose names appear on the Acknowledgments pages,
read the manuscript sections that referred to the people
closest to them and gave me the benefit of their suggestions and corrections.

It was a privilege for me to know my neighbors
better. I hope it will be for you, too.

ALFRED TAMARIN

OHNGWAYHOHWAY
People of the Land

American Indians have not vanished from the eastern United States, even though many people think that all the original inhabitants have been driven away to the West. The sixteen states along the Atlantic Coast are still the homes of more than 115,000 Indians, members of some sixty tribes or groups. Many speak one of a dozen or more different Indian languages, which are still very much alive.

The Eastern Indians inhabit the large cities of the Atlantic seaboard. They also live in the smaller towns and in the countryside and backwoods areas. Many have homes on special tracts of land called reservations or reserves, which have been retained by the Indians through treaties that they signed with the government of the United States or with one of the individual states. These reservations are all that remain of the vast coastal areas once occupied by the Indians.

The United States has grown and developed in great surges westward. Settlement washed over the Eastern Indians like a gigantic wave, leaving them isolated and forgotten. Their numbers had been reduced by countless wars with white settlers. They had been weakened by hardship and destroyed by disease. Many had been unable to withstand the pressure of the colonists and had migrated, willingly or not, to the other side of the Mississippi River. So many Indians had disappeared that it was generally believed that the East was no longer the home of its original inhabitants.

The truth, however, is that many Indians stayed in the East despite every effort to make them move away. Over the years their numbers have increased, so that today there are almost as many Indians living in the East as there were when the first white settlers arrived. In the ten years between 1960 and 1970 the Indian population in the sixteen Atlantic states increased by over 41,000. If that rate of increase continues, there will soon be more Indians along the Atlantic seaboard than ever before.

The name *Indian* is relatively new in the history of America's native people. Before explorers from Europe came upon North and South America, the inhabitants of the two continents called themselves by simple, direct names, most of them meaning "the people," "the men," or "the first men." Some names referred to the sun and other aspects of nature; for example, both *Wampanoag* and *Abnaki* meant "people of the sunrise," or eastern people. Some described natural landmarks, such as the name *Mashpee*, which means "great waters." Other names referred to customs unique to certain groups, such as the Iroquois of New York, who called themselves the *Ho-De-No-Sau-Nee*, or "we people of longhouses." Still others were labels branded on tribes by their enemies, as with a Connecticut tribe whose warlike ways earned it the name of *Pequot*, meaning "destroyers."

Today the Onondaga, an Iroquois nation in central New York, has provided a name that is being used by American Indians—*Ohngwayhohway*, which means "people of the land."

The name *Indian* began with Christopher Columbus, who did not realize that he had discovered what was a new world to the people of Europe. Columbus

ALGONQUIAN—Delaware Indian, wearing headdress and feathers of Eastern tribes.

mistakenly thought that he had arrived at the islands of the East Indies, and he consequently named the native people *Indians*. The people had no idea that they had been lumped together under a single new name, nor did they know that their homeland had also been given a new name—*America*, in honor of an Italian explorer, Amerigo Vespucci.

Every European nation that tried to establish colonies on the Atlantic Coast became involved with the Indians. In Florida the original inhabitants had to deal with the Spanish; in the Middle Atlantic states, with the Swedish; in New York, with the Dutch and the French; and all along the coast, with the English. Some of the encounters were violent; Columbus enslaved countless Indians, whom he carried off to Europe. Other Spanish explorers took Indians captive, branded them on the cheek, and forced them to tend their enslavers' horses. Ponce de Leon's search for a fountain of youth in Florida ended with the Spanish explorer's death from an Indian arrow. Other meetings were friendly; the Pilgrims from England would probably never have survived their first New England winter at Plymouth had they not received gifts of food from the Indians.

As more and more ships brought settlers to New England, feelings between the Indians and the new colonists grew angrier and deadlier. The Indians felt themselves being pushed off their homelands, and they eventually resisted. In 1675, just half a century after the Pilgrims landed, an Indian revolt was led by Pometacom, the second son of Massasoit, the Indian sachem, or chief, who first greeted the Pilgrims at Plymouth Rock. Pometacom became known as King Philip, and the war he led, called King Philip's War, proved a losing battle for the Indians. Their attempt to regain their tribal land was drowned in blood.

When the Europeans first began to colonize the Atlantic coastal regions, more than 100 Indian tribes had their homes in the area. That number has been reduced to about thirty recognized tribes. There may be an equal number who claim Indian ancestry, but whose history has not yet been established.

The Indian tribes in the East belong to different language families and have different origins, social structures, and religious beliefs. Their languages fall into four major categories: the Algonquian, the Iroquois, the Sioux, and the Muskogee. The Algonquian-speaking Indians live throughout New England, in several parts of Long Island, and throughout the Middle Atlantic states as far south as the Carolinas. The Iroquois speakers are in New York, southern Canada, and the Carolinas; once they were also in Virginia and Georgia. A Sioux-speaking people live in North and South Carolina, and two Muskogean language groups are in Florida.

In addition to speaking different languages, the Indians on the Atlantic Coast lived in varied kinds of societies. Their basic differences were reflected in the ways the tribes were organized, in their family patterns and social customs. When the Algonquians were first

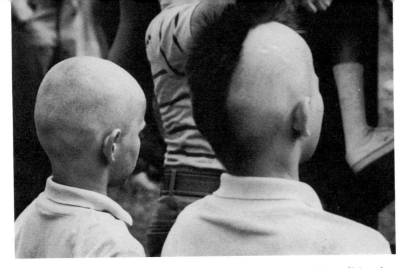

IROQUOIS—Two youthful members of the Six Nations with traditional hair styles.

encountered by the Europeans, for example, the Indians were forest dwellers, who moved with the seasons. They hunted game and gathered roots and wild berries and had only the earliest experience with corn raising. On the other hand, the Iroquois were found already living in settled communities, growing sizable crops in regular fields. Some of these tribal variations have continued into the lives of the people to this day.

Eastern Indians differ today in their religious beliefs, just as they did in the past. Many of the tribes were quickly converted to Christianity. In northern Maine French Catholic priests and nuns still exert strong influence over the Indians. In New England and New York Protestant ministers and missionaries urged the Indians to convert. Some tribes responded to the teachings of the Quakers, and one tribe accepted Mormon beliefs. At the same time, other Indian tribes refused to give up the traditional beliefs of their forefathers. Many still observe their ancient religious customs and faith.

Unlike any other Americans, many Indians live under the terms of treaties signed with the government of the United States or under agreements made with one of the early American colonies or states. These treaties or pacts generally promised payment for tribal lands that were being surrendered and guaranteed the Indians homes on specific reservations. There were usually provisions for health care, education, social services, roads, and other needs.

Reservations for Eastern Indians exist in Maine, Connecticut, New York, Virginia, North Carolina, and Florida. Many of the eastern reservations have services supported by the states in which they are located, but some reserves in New York, North Carolina, and Florida are linked to the Bureau of Indian Affairs in Washington, D.C. In other Atlantic states the reservations that were set up years ago have been dissolved or terminated. However, even outside the reservations, Indians continue to live in closely knit communities in Rhode Island, Massachusetts, New Jersey, Maryland, Delaware, and North and South Carolina.

It is not always easy to recognize an Indian reservation. A superhighway may pass through with no indication that it is built on Indian land. An unobtrusive sign along a minor roadway may announce a reservation nearby; the road may become a little rougher, since it usually is the last public highway in the area to be repaired. The houses along the roadside may appear less prosperous, the lawns less trim, and the fields less tended. The area will not seem very different from many other struggling back-country sections.

The people in Indian communities often live under very difficult conditions. Money and services due them under the terms of their treaties are not always enough to provide for the needs of the people. Social services decline. Prices fluctuate, usually upward. Pieces of reservation land get sliced off to make way for a road, a power line, or a dam. One reservation lost thousands of acres under water that was backed up by a dam miles away.

SIOUX—Elder of the Catawbas of South Carolina.

Yet, despite their many difficulties, most Indians cherish their unique status and take pride in their group unity. They have a strong feeling for their treaties, which have helped to preserve their special relationships with other Indians. They are eager to maintain their distinctiveness and to pass their Indianness along to their children. So highly do they value their identity that they are determined to preserve their customs and beliefs despite the extreme pressure on every side for them to change and become part of the mass of other Americans. This tribal feeling is especially strong among the Eastern Indians who live in closely knit communities and on reservations recognized by state or federal governments.

There are other groups in the East who have great difficulty in proving that they are Indians, even to themselves. The eastern states were settled in so short a time that many Indian communities were pushed aside and submerged without leaving any adequate historical traces. In some instances they survived, hidden in forgotten corners, overlooked by the new settlers. These isolated people, with no clear record to prove their Indian ancestry, are called ''social isolates.''

Descendants of these isolated groups survive today. Some call themselves Indian; others are not sure what they are. There are approximately seventy such communities in remote rural areas throughout the eastern states, ranging in population from less than 10 to more than 30,000. The people have no special social or legal status, are usually extremely poor, and often suffer from severe discrimination by their neighbors.

What it is that identifies a person as an Indian is still generally misunderstood. Since there are no people in all the world who have truly pure bloodlines, looking for racial purity is not only a mistake, but also false and harmful. Anthropologists, sociologists, and other writers for statistical and sociological purposes commonly consider any person with one thirty-seconds of Indian blood an Indian. The 1970 census of the Indian population is based on self-identifying data—that is, on the way in which people listed themselves or their fathers.

Indian communities can appear exactly like every other community around them and still be Indian. The people can vary in skin, hair, and eye coloring, with some being dark and straight-haired and others fair and blue-eyed. Yet all are Indian.

To determine whether a community is Indian, the following questions should be asked. Do the people themselves consider themselves Indian? Do any of the people show facial and body characteristics known to be American Indian? Do the people live in a community with well-defined limits, separated from other surrounding communities?

Some social isolate communities show very definite evidence of an Indian past, which must be accepted. Others claim to be Indian, but no historical evidence has yet been discovered to prove the connection. The difference is more than academic, particularly to the

MUSKOGEE—Woman and child, members of the Miccosukee Seminoles in colorful tribal dress.

people in the community. If they have an accepted Indian history, they are eligible for certain social benefits granted to Indians, and they generally enjoy increased self-esteem. More study of the other isolated groups is required, for it is quite probable that many of their claims to an Indian lineage will still be proved historically valid.

Traditional Indian values differ from those of non-Indians. Some prominent Indian educators have compared the two viewpoints in this way:

The Indian thinks of himself as a member of a group—a family, a clan, a tribe, and finally a nation. He says "we," not "I." Yet he can maintain his individuality and not become lost in a group or a crowd.

Basically he does not consider himself the master of the earth. All the elements in nature—the birds, the animals, the rivers, the woods—are his equals. His inclination is to change himself and his habits, rather than to try to alter the natural world.

If he lives on a reservation, he owns the land as a member of the group. The fields, woods, mountains, and streams belong to all of the tribe. As an individual, he may use what he needs. The land, like the air, is available to him, and he has no concept of the earth as someone's exclusive property, to be bought or sold at will.

In his Indian world he finds no social classes. Everyone lives on the same level. The chief is the first among equals, but has no special privileges.

The Indian does what he can do in the best way that he knows. He will make every effort to be as fast, as strong, and as agile as he can, just to do his utmost. He will work long and hard to win as a group or team member, but he is not primarily motivated to outdo anyone else, to beat any competitors. This noncompetitive spirit can become a serious handicap to him in the world outside the reservation.

Within tribal society the Indian is known by his fellows for what he is, not for what he does to make a living. His work is not a way of life; he has a job, not a career. Only the exceptional person works to become something—a mechanic, an engineer, a doctor.

If he is a craftsman working within his own society, he makes many things—baskets, pottery, canoe paddles—for use, rather than for sale. Quality is more important than quantity or price.

Within Indian society he regards the present as more significant than the future. Because today is more important to him than tomorrow, he is willing to share whatever he has, confident that Nature will always provide. He prefers thrift for short-range plans to self-sacrifice for long-range goals.

Despite all of their differences, the Indian and non-Indian worlds have lived side by side for many years. Each has exerted strong influences over the other. For a long time non-Indians considered the Indian way of life savage, primitive, and of little value. Constant pressure was put on the Indians to give up their traditional ways. Many Indians did. Some tried and found the changeover difficult. Others refused to change.

But even while the non-Indian world was dismissing Indian ways as valueless, it was adopting many Indian ideas and developments. It was accepting such Indian items as tobacco, rubber balls, American cotton, corn, beans, potatoes, tomatoes, pumpkins, squash, maple syrup, chocolate, popcorn, chewing gum, and peanuts. Other familiar items adopted from the Indians are the toboggan, the moccasin, the turkey, tapioca, wild rice, and the guinea pig. Modern medicine accepted such Indian medicine men's drugs as quinine, cocaine, witch hazel, arnica, oil of wintergreen, ipecac, petroleum jelly, and cascara sagrada.

More important, however, was the change in human values that came over the settlers in North America after their experiences with the Indians. For the settlers, whether they realized it or not, were as much influenced by the Indians as the Indians were by the newcomers from across the sea. In fact, many qualities now considered part of our American heritage are of Indian origin.

In America the Indian was his own master. He was neither a slave nor a serf, nor did he own or control any. He was neither submissive to authority nor intolerant of it. He was generally free, independent, and self-reliant. He displayed qualities that were not common among the first American settlers, who came from lands of kings and serfs. Some of the first colonists were fleeing religious persecution; some were indentured servants; some were convicts. In the freer air of America the early Europeans found the independence of the Indians very attractive.

The political form of the United States owes much to the inspiration of Indian forms of government. In Europe there were no democracies joining together free and equal states in a federal union. Europe had no government for the new America to copy. The Indians, however, did have such a model—the Iroquois Indians in central New York State. The League of the Iroquois consisted of a central council made up of the chiefs of five (later six) Indian nations, all free and equal. The Iroquois form of government was known to Benjamin Franklin and other early American leaders, and it helped inspire them to create the new United States, with a federal government uniting thirteen colonies as free and equal states.

In addition to having ideals of freedom and equality, Americans expected their government to work, to be practical, even if everyone did not always agree. This idea, possibly based on another Indian quality, was embodied in an expression that crept into the English language from the speech of the Choctaw Indians, who once lived in Alabama and Mississippi. The term is the very popular "okay"—which to the Indians meant, not that all was correct, but rather that all parties had reached the point where they could agree, even if the agreement was not absolutely perfect.

MAINE

The state of Maine is still the home of approximately 2,200 Indians. Most of them belong to four tribes of Algonquian-speaking people—the Passamaquoddy, the Penobscot, the Malecite, and the Micmac.

During the American Revolution Passamaquoddy and Penobscot Indians fought alongside the New England colonists against the soldiers of Great Britain. After the war American settlers spread out and occupied most of the territory of the two tribes. The land that was left to the Indians was established as a reservation by the state of Massachusetts under the terms of a treaty signed in 1792. When Maine, originally part of Massachusetts, became a separate state in 1820, it assumed the obligations due the Indians within its borders.

In 1965 Maine became one of the few states to have a full-time Department of Indian Affairs. The department is headed by a commissioner, who has a deputy to assist him. These officials may be Maine Indians.

PASSAMAQUODDY
"spearers of the pollack"

About 600 Passamaquoddy Indians in Maine live on state reservations. An equal number reside away from the reserves. One group lives on a reserve near the easternmost point in the United States, where the Atlantic Ocean cuts inland to form Passamaquoddy Bay. About 100 acres in size, the reservation, with its village of Pleasant Point, is tucked between a highway and a single-track railway line. Both the highway and the rail line are on land belonging to the Passamaquoddy Reserve. Both were built without asking permission of the Indians.

Cars constantly zoom along the highway, but the lone railroad track usually lies empty. Passenger trains no longer run on the line, and long strings of freight cars pass through only now and then. The tracks, skirting the shore of the bay, have become a place for Indian children to play and fish.

In the village of Pleasant Point are a church and a schoolhouse. Clustered around these buildings are the homes of the Indians. Some of the houses are trim, sparkling with fresh paint; others show signs of poverty and neglect. Very few trees have been left standing along the streets.

Far off on the horizon to the east, a smudge of smoke marks the location of the newer society that has

Passamaquoddy children on the empty railroad that skirts
Passamaquoddy Bay.

moved into the Passamaquoddy homeland. The smoke
rises from non-Indian homes and factories in Eastport,
the easternmost city in the United States.

A second group of Passamaquoddy Indians have
another reservation in Maine about fifty miles inland.
This reserve, called Indian Township, covers 18,000
acres of forest land along the banks of Big Lake and
Lowey's Lake. Most of the Indians live in two settled

areas—Peter Dana's Point and The Strip. Both settlements are squeezed between a highway and the clear, cold lake waters.

The Passamaquoddy are people of the forests. Many of the men are employed as lumbermen or workers in nearby paper pulp mills. Some men act as guides for hunters and fishermen.

The name *Passamaquoddy* reveals the tribe's ties to the sea, for in the Algonquian language the word means "spearers of the pollack." The pollack, a dark, shiny fish related to the codfish, was once plentiful in the waters off the coast of Maine. The name *Passamaquoddy* also reflects the tribal kinship to the Algonquians—a name that means "at the place of spearing fish or eels."

Recently an alphabet was developed for the Passamaquoddy language, and it became a written language for the first time. Now Passamaquoddy children can learn to read and write, as well as speak, their native tongue.

The children attend their own schools on the Indian Township Reserve and the Pleasant Point Reservation. The schools are taught by Catholic nuns, a tradition dating to the early eighteenth century when Catholic France was an important European influence in the area.

The Passamaquoddy elect six members from each reserve to a joint council, which acts for both tribal settlements. They also elect a governor for each reservation and a representative to the state legislature. The Indian representative cannot vote on the legislation that may affect his people.

From Passamaquoddy Bay the boundary line between the United States and Canada follows the St. Croix River to Grand Lake and then goes north, straight across the land. The international border cuts through Indian territory, for centuries the home of the Malecite Indians, who now number about 600.

Treeless under the Maine sun lies Pleasant Point, a reserve of the Passamaquoddy. On the horizon a smoke cloud hangs over Eastport, across Passamaquoddy Bay.

MALECITE
"broken talkers"

The *Malecite* name was derived from a word in the Algonquian language of a neighboring tribe, who called the Maine Indians "broken talkers."

There are no reservations or special communities for the Malecite in Maine. Their homes are scattered throughout the potato-growing country of Aroostook County, which lies along the United States-Canadian boundary; their children attend schools with non-Indian children.

The Indian population in Aroostook County fluctuates with the potato crop. At harvest time Canadian Indians cross the border to work in the fields. Some stay in the United States and try to find work to support themselves through the winter and spring. At most the number of Malecite in Maine may reach a few hundred. Perhaps half of them still speak their native Indian tongue.

A one-lane bridge links the Penobscot reserve on Indian Island with the mainland.

MICMAC
"allies"

A few Micmac Indians also live in Aroostook County. Their name is derived from an Algonquian word meaning "allies," reflecting their alliance with the French settlers of Canada. They were also known as the "porcupine Indians" because of their skill in using porcupine quills to decorate moccasins and clothing.

▞▚▞

PENOBSCOT
"falling-down place"

▞▚▞

The Penobscot Indians have an estimated population of 800, including tribal members both in and out of Maine. The Indians in the state live on an island in the Penobscot River near the rapids above the city of Oldtown. The rapids are the "falling down place" referred to in the ancient Wabanaki-Algonquian word that gave the tribe its name. The Wabanaki were at one time another tribe of Maine Indians in the Algonquian group.

The Penobscot settlement in the middle of the river is known as Indian Island. It is one of 146 islands that stretch upriver for seventy miles, covering 4,400 acres. All of the islands make up the Penobscot Indian Reserve, but only Indian Island is inhabited.

The Penobscot, like other Maine Indians, were expert rivermen. They were known for their ability to make and use the long, lightweight boats associated with Indian lore, the birch-bark canoe. They were also skillful at carving the wooden paddles used to propel the canoes.

Modern Penobscot men have not forgotten the tradition of their ancestors. Some elders of the tribe continue to be skilled wood-carvers and paddle-makers. Sometimes Penobscot men are employed in an Oldtown factory that manufactures canoes and canoe paddles.

For many years Indian Island could be reached only by boat or canoe. Eventually a small ferryboat was put into service to shuttle between the island and the mainland. The Penobscot, however, rarely used the ferry. They preferred crossing in their own boats or canoes. The ferry carried primarily non-Indian passengers and supplies for the people on Indian Island.

In recent times a bridge was built to replace the ferry. The bridge is narrow, with only a single lane for cars and trucks, but it has allowed the Penobscot to drive their own cars back and forth between the mainland and their homes on the island.

With the city of Oldtown so easy to reach, the Penobscot began to mingle more with their non-Indian neighbors. The intermingling has had some good effects in widening the horizon of the tribespeople, but it has also broken down some of their traditional ways. The Penobscot language has almost disappeared. It is no longer taught to the children, and only a few elders of the tribe can still remember it. Recently, however, efforts have been made to write down and preserve the ancient language.

A public school on Indian Island offers classes from the kindergarten to the sixth grade. Upper grades and high school classes are available to Penobscot children in the public schools on the mainland.

The Penobscot elect their own governor and council. They also elect a representative to the Maine legislature; however, he has no vote.

Maine's 1970 Indian population of 2,195 represents an increase in ten years of almost 300 people. This trend has been going on for many years, for the number of Indians in the state has doubled since 1930 and almost tripled since 1900.

MASSACHUSETTS

The state of Massachusetts owes its name to its original Indian inhabitants. In the Algonquian language the word *Massachusetts* means "at the great hills" or "blue hills." The reference is to the highlands around Boston, which were once the homeland of an Indian tribe known as the Massachusetts.

The number of Indians living in Massachusetts today is about 4,500. The total includes Indians who came from other states, as well as descendants of the original inhabitants. The state has no special governmental agency for the Indians within its borders.

Approximately 2,000 Indians in Massachusetts are members of the Wampanoag, Nauset, or Mashpee tribes. Today's Wampanoag and Nauset are descended

WAMPANOAG
"people of the sunrise"

from the Indians who, led by their chief, Massasoit, greeted the Pilgrims at Plymouth Rock in 1620.

As their name indicated, the Wampanoag, or "people of the sunrise," lived along the eastern shores of New England. The Nauset name, meaning "bended land," described their home on Cape Cod, which juts out into the Atlantic Ocean like a bent elbow.

NAUSET
"bended land"

Today the Wampanoag and Nauset also live on Martha's Vineyard, an island off the southern coast of Massachusetts about ten miles out to sea. The island received its name twenty years before the Pilgrims began settling the mainland. An English sea captain named it for his granddaughter, Martha, after he saw the flourishing grape vineyards there.

Along the southern tip of Martha's Vineyard are great cliffs, composed of various colored clays. They have been designated as a registered national landmark. At the top of the cliffs is the township of Gay Head, about 3,000 acres in extent and the site of approximately 200 Indian homes.

Towering cliffs at Gay Head, Martha's Vineyard, near land of the Wampanoag.

Gay Head was an official Indian reservation until 1870. The area was separated from the rest of Martha's Vineyard by a ditch four feet deep and planted with thorns. The purpose of the thorns, some said, was to keep intruders out of the reservation; others said it was to keep the Indians in. When the reservation was dissolved, the present township was created. All that remains of the former reservation lands are marshes where wild cranberries once grew. Cranberry picking was an important source of income for the Gay Head inhabitants until a hurricane ruined the berry bushes.

Living so close to the sea, the Wampanoag and Nauset of Gay Head are skillful boatmen and fishermen. Their catch is usually lobster, scallops, and herring.

Indian tradition at Gay Head is deeply involved with the sea. Tribal legends tell of a giant named Moshup, who befriended the poor and the helpless. In one tale Moshup, seeing that his people were hungry, scoops up a great whale from the ocean for them to eat. Another tale describes how he helps an Indian girl who has no dowry with which to get a husband, by emptying the ashes from his pipe into the sea, thereby creating the island of Nantucket as a bridal gift.

Like all Massachusetts townships, Gay Head is governed by a board of selectmen. In Gay Head the officials are usually Indians. The non-Indians in Gay Head send their children to the same schools as the Indians. The ancient Indian language is no longer used.

MASHPEE
"great waters"

On the mainland of Massachusetts live the Mashpee Indians, who are descendants of the Wampanoag and the Nauset. The "great waters" that gave the Mashpee their name are Mashpee Lake and the river that flows from it. The Indians inhabit several townships along the southern coast of Cape Cod, which once were Indian reservations. Most of the officials of the townships are Indians.

The Mashpee also have three communities in Barnstable County: Mashpee, Yarmouth, and Waquoit. Another group lives near the city of Fall River. Standing in the township of Mashpee is the oldest Indian church in the eastern United States. It is still actively used as a house of worship.

The Mashpee communities also include non-Indians, whose children attend the local schools. The ancient tribal language is no longer spoken.

The Mashpee have encouraged the development of several non-Indian business enterprises around their communities. Some small industrial plants and a sizable retirement village have been built within the townships. The construction work provided many job opportunities for local Indian men. The Mashpee are also employed in many of the recreational facilities along the shores of Cape Cod and on the off-shore islands. Before the berry bushes were destroyed in a hurricane, many Mashpee men also worked in the nearby cranberry bogs.

A tiny plot of land in Massachusetts still clings to the status of being an Indian reservation. The land, just

Originally built 300 years ago, Indian church at Mashpee is still in use.

under twelve acres in size, is located immediately outside the town of Grafton, near Worcester. It has always been the home of the Nipmuc Indians. The tribe's name means "fresh-water fishing place" in an Algonquian tongue.

The land near Grafton was set aside as the Hassanamisco Reservation in 1927. Its location is signaled by a marker put up along the highway years earlier, which reads: *These four and one-half [sic] acres have never belonged to the white man, having been set aside in 1728 as an Indian reservation by the forty proprietors who purchased the praying Indian town of Hassanamesit.* The name, spelled either of two ways, means "a place of many small stones."

The Nipmuc were the second Indian tribe in Massachusetts to accept the Christian religious beliefs of the European settlers. One of the early leaders of the Nipmuc earned the name of James the Printer, because he helped translate the Bible into his Algonquian tongue and assisted in its printing. The Nipmuc language is no longer spoken.

The tiny Hassanamisco Reservation is not given official status by the Commonwealth of Massachusetts. The one house on the grounds is not inhabited all year round. The land has been passed down from generation to generation of Indians in the form of a trust for many of the Nipmucs, who have scattered throughout the United States. Their number has been estimated at several hundred, though an exact figure is impossible to determine.

A few of the Nipmuc still live in nearby communities, where they work at various occupations. They are governed by the same laws and officials as their neighbors, and their children attend the same schools as their non-Indian friends.

Massachusetts' 4,475 Indians in 1970 represented more than double the number of Indians in the state in 1960, five times the number in 1930, and almost eight times the number since the beginning of the twentieth century. More than three-quarters of the Indians live in the state's larger urban areas. None yet reside on an area of over 200 acres in the Freetown-Fall River State Forest that has been designated an Indian reservation.

NEW HAMPSHIRE

In New Hampshire, near the city of Manchester, a few surviving members of the once-powerful tribe of Pennacook Indians can still be found.

The name *Pennacook* means "at the bottom of the hill" or "down hill." The state's Indians number only about 360. This figure represents more than a twofold increase in the ten years between 1960 and 1970, and it is six times New Hampshire's Indian population in 1930 and sixteen times the population in 1900. At least half of the Indians in the state live in its urban areas.

The original Indian inhabitants of New Hampshire were closely related to the tribes of Maine. The Pennacook—meaning "at the bottom of the hill" or simply "down hill"—were members of the Algonquian lan-

PENNACOOK
"at the bottom of the hill"

guage family, linked intimately to the Penobscot, the Passamaquoddy, and the Malecite Indians nearby. In the seventeenth century, after several bloody encounters with settlers from Europe, most of the original Pennacook Indians of New Hampshire abandoned their homes and joined communities in Canada. Some wandered westward into the valley of the upper Hudson River, where they settled for a while.

New Hampshire has no special reservation lands for the Indians, and no special governmental agency exists to look after them and their needs.

VERMONT

Vermont is the home of over 200 American Indians, probably from tribes throughout the East as well as the rest of the country. There are no official tribal groupings registered in the state and no state agency concerned with Indian affairs.

Vermont's modern Indian citizens are not descended from the state's original inhabitants. Before the area was settled by Europeans, Indians from surrounding states made their homes in the Vermont hills and valleys. Abnakis from Maine settled along one of the eastern rivers. Bands of Mahicans from New York state hunted in the southwestern and western sections and probably set up temporary settlements. The eastern edges of Vermont were occupied by Pennacook from

New Hampshire and the southern parts by Indians from Massachusetts.

The 229 Indians listed in Vermont in 1970 represent a fourfold increase since 1960 and a sixfold increase since 1930. In 1900 only five Indians were listed in the state's population. Three-quarters of the Vermont Indians live in rural areas.

RHODE ISLAND

Rhode Island is still the home of the Narragansett Indians, who have never moved far from the land of their ancestors. Most of the Indians in the state live near the city of Kingston, along the western shores of Narragansett Bay. The bay cuts deeply into the southern coast of New England, almost dividing Rhode Island in two and probably accounting for the tribal name *Narragansett*, which means "people of the small point."

Narragansett Bay was a secure harbor for the frail European sailing ships that brought explorers of many nations to the Americas. The Narragansett Indians were among the first to be encountered by Europeans and described in early writings. In 1524 the navigator Giovanni da Verrazzano came upon the tribe and wrote

NARRAGANSETT
"people of the small point"

about them to his patron, the king of France.

Approximately a century later, in 1620, the Pilgrims landed at Plymouth, followed ten years later by the Puritans, who founded the second English colony in Massachusetts at Boston. One Boston colonist, Roger Williams, contended that the settlers could not take land from the Indians without proper payment. Williams' critical position was very unpopular, and in 1636 he was forced to flee. He escaped Boston through the snow-covered forest and was rescued by the Narragansett Indians. Later Roger Williams founded a new colony, which he named Rhode Island. He was always interested in his Indian neighbors, for whom he put in writing the Narragansett language. He even had the Bible translated into the Indian tongue.

The Narragansett language, thus one of the earliest Indian tongues to be set down on paper, is no longer a living language. None of the people can speak or write it today.

For more than fifty years after the Pilgrims landed at Plymouth, the Indians of New England remained friendly to the English settlers. By 1675, however, with probably more colonists than Indians in the area, King Philip's War was launched to try to stop the colonists from pushing the Indians out of their homeland. Philip, or Pometacom, tried to rally all the Indians of New England for a united effort that would drive the colonists away.

In December 1675 Philip was with the Narragansett Indians, recruiting them for his crusade. He was in a walled Indian village in the Great Swamp, near South Kingston, when he was surrounded and trapped by colonial soldiers from Boston and Plymouth. The village was burned to the ground, and all of its inhabitants were captured or killed. The Narragansett tribe itself was smashed and scattered. Many Indian men, women, and children were sold into slavery, including Philip's wife and son. Philip himself was later captured and executed.

Narragansett Indian Church, built by the Indians, still on tribal land in Rhode Island.

The site of the Great Swamp Fight is marked by a granite column, which bears this inscription: *The Narragansett Indians Made Their Last Stand in King Philip's War and Were Crushed by the United Forces of the Massachusetts, Connecticut, and Plymouth Colonies in the Great Swamp Fight.* Though the bloody fighting took place on Rhode Island soil, Roger Williams' colony did not participate in the attack.

Every year Indians from throughout the United States gather at the Great Swamp monument. They join hands and form a giant circle around the granite marker. Slowly the circle moves around the stone monolith, and the Indians pelt the column with flowers in tribute to their fallen ancestors.

The defeat and death of Philip ended forever the power of the Indians in southern New England. The original Narragansett tribe, practically wiped out by the Great Swamp Fight, managed to survive only by the addition of new members from other Indian tribes in the area. New chiefs were named for the new tribe. The chiefs were called Ninigret and were given the titles of king or queen by the English colonists. The royal titles were passed down by the chiefs to their children.

Ceremonies crowning the Ninigret are still celebrated by the Narragansett. A recent festival honored the 200th anniversary of the coronation of the last of the Ninigret, Queen Esther, who was crowned in 1770. She did not have any children to succeed her. The reenactment of her coronation was held at Coronation Rock, on a farm near Charlestown. In the pageant the queen marched proudly to the rock, followed by an Indian warrior and a column of children dressed in uniforms representing a royal guard of honor.

Thirty-three years after the death of King Philip, the Narragansett settled down on a reserve, which covered almost 1,000 acres. They remained on the

Gaunt granite memorial marks the Indians' defeat at the Great Swamp Fight.

Narragansett Indians celebrate anniversary of their last Rhode Island chief.

Rhode Island reservation for 170 years.

During all that time, however, the Narragansett lived under very difficult conditions. They could not establish satisfactory schools and other necessary facilities on the reservation. As a result, in 1879–80 the Indians decided that they would fare better if the reservation were dissolved. Nine hundred and twenty-two acres of the reservation were sold for $5,000, which was divided among the members of the tribe, each receiving a small amount. Without their reservation, the people became ordinary citizens of the state, with no special schools, employment, or political position.

Two acres of the Narragansett Reservation near Charlestown were not sold with all the rest. These two acres are still tribally owned. On them are a community house, called the Narragansett Long House, and a church with an Indian minister. The church was built of fieldstone by the Narragansett, many of whom through the years have become expert stonecutters and masons.

The sale of their reservation did not put an end to the tribal life of the Narragansett. The people stayed together, keeping their community feelings alive, and in 1934 they organized as the Narragansett Tribe, Incorporated.

Over the years the tribe has grown, and it now numbers about 1,400, according to the 1970 census. In 1960 the population count listed almost 500 fewer Indians in Rhode Island; in 1930 there were just over 300, and in 1900, only thirty-five. Eighty-five percent of the Indians in the state today live in the cities.

Rhode Island has no state agency to provide special supervision over Indian affairs.

CONNECTICUT

The state of Connecticut gets its name from the Connecticut River, which to the area's original Algonquian Indians meant the "long, tidal flow river."

Approximately 2,200 Indians are listed as residents of the state today. Some are descendants of the native Algonquians. Others are members of tribes in other states who have come to Connecticut in recent times.

The original Indians of Connecticut found themselves involved in conflicts even before the early white settlers moved into the fertile valley of the Connecticut River.

A related Algonquian tribe, which came to be known as the Pequot, or "destroyers," was driven out of New York by the Iroquois. The Pequots pushed

▀▀▀

PEQUOT
"destroyers" or "invaders"

▀▀▀

their way down the Connecticut River Valley until they reached the southern shores of the state bordering Long Island Sound. Along the way many of the local tribes were forcibly taken under the wing of the more warlike Pequots.

The Indians in Connecticut also had to contend with powerful neighbors in what is now New York State—the unrelated Iroquois-speaking Mohawks. The Mohawk had probably driven the Pequots out of New York, forcing them to push their way into Connecticut. The Mohawk themselves often made demands on the Connecticut Indians for quantities of wampum, the valued white and purple beads made from clam shells. The beads were cut and pierced and then strung together to make sacred wampum belts.

More trouble came to the Indians of Connecticut when the area became one of the earliest New England states to be colonized by Europeans. The Dutch from New York were the first to sail up the Connecticut River and establish colonies in the river valley. The British from Massachusetts followed almost immediately afterwards. Rivalry between the colonists sprang up at once, and the neighboring Indians found themselves caught in the middle. Some turned to the British for help and protection; others allied themselves with the Dutch.

While the Dutch were buying land from the Indians in the Connecticut River Valley early in the 1600s, they were recording their purchases with official deeds, written in a language that the Indians could neither read nor understand. The deeds of purchase were then registered as permanent records in the colony's books. At first the Indians did not grasp the significance of these sheets of paper, marked with signs and symbols that were meaningless to them. They did not realize that they were giving up to strangers exclusive rights to land on which their people had lived for centuries. But they soon discovered that this was what they had done, that only the strange newcomers now had the right to roam across the land, to hunt on it, and to fish in its streams and rivers.

The rivalry between the Dutch and the British kept the Connecticut Indians in a constant turmoil until 1664, when the Dutch relinquished their rights in the area to the British. At the same time the Dutch settlement of New Amsterdam became the English colony of New York.

Before this time, however, in 1638, just eighteen years after the first settlers had arrived in New England, one of the earliest of the colonial wars took place in Connecticut. The English colonists undertook an expedition against the Indians in what is called the Pequot War. The Pequot, living in a walled village near Mystic, were surrounded and their homes destroyed. Most of the Indian men, women, and children were killed in the battle.

A few of the Pequot escaped destruction and scattered into the forests for safety. The colonists, with their Indian allies, pursued the survivors so relentlessly that the Pequot were in danger of extinction. The English then took it upon themselves to rescue the remaining Pequots, who were then settled on reserves. At first these reservations were extensive, but through the years the land has been whittled away and the number of Indians on the reserves has greatly decreased.

Two state reservations for the Pequot remain near the village of Ledyard, just outside of Norwich. One, now called the Eastern Pequot Reserve, consists of 224 acres. Not far away is the Western Pequot Reserve, which covers 184 acres. A few Pequot descendants still have homes or summer camps on the reservations. These homesites are tax free, but enjoy no other special privileges.

According to official state sources, there are about thirteen surviving members of the Pequot tribe in Connecticut. They no longer speak a native language and exhibit none of the original Algonquian social customs. Most live in regular communities and send their children to public schools.

MOHEGAN
"wolf people"

The Indians who sided with the English against the Pequot were closely related Algonquians, whose name was changed to Mohegans, or "wolf people." Their chief at the time was named Uncas; the town of Uncasville, near New London, is named after him. The Mohegans settled on a reservation located along the Thames River near the city of Norwich. The reserve continued as Indian territory until 1860. Thirty-five Mohegan Indians still live nearby, some on the land that was once part of the reservation. The total number of Mohegans in Connecticut now has been estimated at about 200. Some live in the capital city of Hartford; others have moved to other states and even to foreign countries.

Chief Harold Tantaquidgeon's mark, symbolizing four winds, compass points, and ancestors.

SCATICOOK or SCHAGHTICOKE
"mouth of the river"

A few survivors of the Pequot War managed to find refuge in western Connecticut. There they joined with the Scaticook, or Schaghticoke, Indians, who were living on a 400-acre reserve near the New York State border at Kent. Officially there are now only three residents on the reserve, but the tribe has recently elected a new chief, or sachem, and planned a powwow, or ceremonial meeting, on their territory.

Connecticut's fourth official Indian reserve is the smallest in existence. It consists of a single house on one lot. The house is occupied by a Pequot family, which has lived on the reserve for several generations. The family now consists of two old people, who may also be linked to the ancient New England tribe, the Paugusett.

The reservation, called the Golden Hill Reserve, is in the town of Trumbull, north of Bridgeport.

The origins of the reservations in Connecticut are buried in files of dusty documents, which have not been examined for many years. The early settlers of the state enacted many laws and set down many regulations regarding the Indians. Today, however, there is no special state agency to look after the needs of Connecticut's original inhabitants. The four reservations are held in trusteeship by the state for "so long as there shall be an Indian to reside on the reservation," according to official statements. The responsibility for managing the reservations has been in the hands of the State Welfare Department since 1941.

The Indians in Connecticut are largely assimilated into non-Indian communities. Seventy-seven percent live in the larger cities of the state, according to the 1970 census. The few Indians on reservations are, for the most part, self-supporting, though the state does help the needier residents, just as it helps other citizens of the state who are eligible for government aid.

The 2,222 Connecticut Indians counted in the 1970 census represent an increase of almost two and a half times since 1960. This is ten times the number listed for 1930 and 1900.

NEW YORK

More Indians live in New York State today than ever before. In the 1970 census they numbered over 28,000 people, giving New York the second largest Indian population of any state along the Atlantic seaboard. New York's Indian population has mounted year after year. It is now nearly two times larger than the 1960 figure, four times the 1930 figure, and five times the 1900 figure.

Indians in New York belong to two of the major language groups on the East Coast: the Iroquois and the Algonquian. The Iroquois-speaking people are in the vast majority.

Almost 70 percent of the Indians in the state live in the cities and surrounding urban areas. Many live and

▀▄▀

IROQUOIS
"real adder people"

▀▄▀

work in Syracuse, Buffalo, and other cities in central New York. A large community of Indians is in Brooklyn. Only about 10,000 Iroquois and 400 Algonquians reside on reservations in the state.

Of the nine reservations in New York, all but one are inhabited. Iroquois people occupy six reserves, which cover 74,898 acres in the central and western parts of the state and an additional 14,640 acres along the St. Lawrence River, across from Canada. The two Algonquian reserves are smaller, covering 60 acres and 300 acres on Long Island.

The Indian lands in New York have not been subject to treaties with the federal government. Only the Seneca of western New York have a continuing relationship with the Bureau of Indian Affairs in Washington because of a dam built within Seneca territory. The state government has undertaken the major responsibility for supplying health, education, and other public and social services to the tribes. However, many of the Iroquois still look to their tribal chiefs for political direction.

Since the establishment of the various reservations, the Indians in New York have taken on many of the ways of their non-Indian neighbors. Both on and off the reservations, they are employed in many of the same jobs as non-Indians—in factories, offices, mines, hospitals, schools. Their children largely attend integrated schools in local school districts, rather than the all-Indian schools that once were conducted on populated reservations; in 1970 only three separate Indian schools,

Dance demonstration by Iroquois chiefs Jacob Ezra Thomas and Eugene Skye. Eagle headdress is from Plains Indians.

with an enrollment of 683, were still in operation in the state. In the face of these and other changes, many of the Iroquois in the state press strongly to preserve their history and heritage.

Originally the Iroquois, migrating from the South and West, established themselves like a wedge in the midst of the earlier Algonquian tribes on the Atlantic seaboard. Some Algonquians were pushed north into New England; others were forced south into New Jersey, Pennsylvania, and Delaware.

The Iroquois were able to overcome the original inhabitants because the newcomers had already become farmers while the Algonquians were still wandering hunters and plant gatherers. The Iroquois established strong walled villages, surrounded by fields in which they grew sizable crops. The result was a division of labor, with Iroquois women tending the fields and Iroquois men doing the hunting and fighting. By growing their own dependable food supply, the Iroquois could form hunting and raiding bands that traveled vast distances throughout the eastern seaboard.

The Iroquois also had the advantage of a strategic network of waterways, which fanned out of their New York heartland in every direction. They could journey west by canoe across Lake Ontario and Lake Erie, as well as down the Allegheny to the Ohio. The St. Lawrence River took them north and east, and the Susquehanna and Delaware rivers were routes south. Also, flowing through the heart of Iroquois country was the Mohawk River, joining the Hudson River to provide a passageway to what is now New York City and the sea.

The network of waterways formed a vast and fertile breeding ground for beaver, whose fur was highly prized by Europeans. As the demand for beaver skins grew, the Iroquois moved swiftly along the rivers in all

Iroquois false face mask, "Old Broken Nose," shown to Donna Thomas by her father, Jacob Ezra Thomas.

directions and took control of the new and profitable commerce.

While the Iroquois men were away hunting food, trapping beaver, or fighting intertribal wars, the women remained at home, rearing the children and tending the fields. Iroquois life traditionally centered about the women. They owned the family homes and household goods, and they had strong influence in all affairs of the tribe, primarily because they named the chiefs. Also, the Iroquois were divided into clans made up of many families, and clan membership passed to children through their mothers rather than their fathers. One reason that women played so prominent a role in Iroquois society may have been the frequent absences of the men. If Iroquois men died in the forest or were killed in battle, there were always the women to carry on the life of the family and the tribe.

Iroquois society was generally relaxed. Rules were not overly strict. A member of the tribe looked to his chief for guidance and heeded him if he agreed. Family life was easygoing and education informal. Iroquois children learned from their elders their duties to family, clan, and tribe. When they reached adolescence, they were sent into the forest to fast for a few days. A boy remained in solitude until he was visited by his spirit, which thereafter became a part of his life. Upon his return to the village, he was ready to assume a man's role in the life of the tribe.

Much of tribal life centered around religion. The ancient Iroquois faith was known as the Longhouse, probably a symbolic reference to the long barracklike bark houses built by the Iroquois and occupied by several related families. Many religious ceremonies were held throughout the year. A number celebrated harvest time and other agricultural events; and the main Iroquois crops of corn, beans, and squash, known as the "three sisters," had special religious significance.

The Iroquois also organized medicine groups and secret societies to fight off illnesses. These secret organizations, such as the Little Water, Otter, Bear, and Eagle societies, still exist. Some of the best known are the False Face societies whose members cover their faces with wooden masks cut from the trunk of a living tree. Before fashioning each mask, the carver apologizes to the tree and burns tobacco as an offering to its spirit. False Face society masks are sacred. Once they are consecrated by a medicine man, they are not seen again except in religious ceremonies. During such ceremonies masked dancers crowd into the houses of fellow Iroquois, scattering ashes over the inhabitants in an effort to prevent illness from striking them in the coming year.

The original League of the Iroquois was made up of five related tribes, or nations: the Mohawk, the Oneida, the Onondaga, the Cayuga, and the Seneca. Early in the eighteenth century a sixth Iroquois tribe, the Tuscarora, came north to New York from the Carolinas and was admitted into the League, making it the Six Nation Confederacy. The Iroquois believed the Confederacy to be sheltered by a symbolic longhouse, which was imagined as occupying the entire central section of New York, stretching for several hundred miles from its eastern gate at the Hudson River to its western portal facing Lake Erie.

The Mohawk were the guardians of the eastern gate of the Iroquois Longhouse. They lived in the valley of the Mohawk River and along the western shore of the upper Hudson River. Across the river was the start of Algonquian territory. The name *Mohawk* means "men of flint," reflecting the tribe's role as warriors, armed with stone points and flint arrowheads. They may well have been responsible for the name *Iroquois*, meaning "real adder," which was given to the original Five Nations.

The Mohawk were probably the first of the Iroquois to be encountered by the early European settlers along the upper Hudson River. Within a few years the Indians found themselves crowded out of central New York. Many moved north toward the St. Lawrence River and Canada, which was then under the control of the French.

MOHAWK
"men of flint"

Eventually a reserve became the home of the Mohawk. It covered almost 40,000 acres along both sides of the St. Lawrence River. When Canada and the United States were separated after the American Revolution, 15,000 acres of the Mohawk reservation remained within the United States. The rest was within the boundaries of Canada. The reservation land that remained inside New York State is called the St. Regis Mohawk Reservation. It also has an Indian name, *Akwesasne*, a Mohawk word meaning "the land where the partridge drums." The Canadian portion of the reserve, covering 23,750 acres near the city of Montreal, is called the Caughnawaga Reservation, its name meaning "rapid or rushing water."

In 1794 a treaty between the United States and Great Britain, called the John Jay Treaty, guaranteed the Indians the right to travel freely back and forth across the international boundary line. Recently, when an international toll bridge was built connecting the American and Canadian mainlands through Cornwall

Mohawk chief Thayendanegea, known as Joseph Brant. From a painting by Charles Willson Peale.

Island in the St. Lawrence River, the Indians insisted that their rights of duty-free passage be respected.

The Mohawk have two tribal political structures. A state-sponsored governmental system has tribal headquarters in Hogansburg, near the Canadian border. In this official system three chiefs and three sub-chiefs are elected every two years. The Six Nations of the Iroquois recognize a second, more traditional organization in which the Mohawk, like the other Iroquois nations, select their own life-time chiefs.

The St. Regis and Caughnawaga Mohawks cooperate in efforts to promote the interests of their communities on both reservations. Commercial and industrial establishments—all under private Indian ownership—include a Mohawk Indian village that attracts tourists; two marinas, one connected with a restaurant and the other with a trailer court; and a construction company.

One group of Mohawk did not leave central New York to live on the St. Regis or Caughnawaga reservations. These Mohawk urged the Iroquois League to support the British against the colonists during the American Revolution. The League pondered the problem, but could not agree upon which side to aid. Each of the Six Nations was left free to decide for itself. The

Mohawk, led by their chief, Thayendanegea, known in English as Joseph Brant, chose to side with the British.

When the British surrendered at the end of the American Revolution, the Mohawk were forced to find new homes outside of the boundaries of the new United States. They ceded their lands within New York and, still led by Brant, settled in Canada, west of Niagara Falls. Near the little town called Brantford, many Mohawk and other Iroquois still inhabit a reservation, known as the Six Nations Reserve.

Many Iroquois traditions have been preserved on the Mohawk reservations. The Mohawk still speak their ancient Iroquois language, and many adhere to traditional Longhouse religious beliefs. Others have been converted to various denominations of Christianity. The Green Corn Ceremony, the ancient Indian feast honoring the ripening of the corn, is still held every year, and basket-weaving is still practiced by both men and women. The men cut the ash trees and prepare the thin wooden strips, which the women plait into baskets.

Work for the Mohawk men has changed since ancient days and yet is similar in one respect. Like their hunting ancestors, Mohawk men today often leave their homes and families on the reservations and travel to find work. Many modern Mohawk find employment on high steel, climbing the dizzying heights of steel skyscrapers and bridge skeletons without hesitation. Mohawk steel construction men are among the most skillful workers in the trade.

Many of the Mohawk steel workers spend weekdays in Brooklyn, where Indians from fifteen states live closely together. On the weekends, however, the Mohawk men drive hundreds of miles to return to their families on the reservations, bringing home their salaries almost as their ancestors once brought home game from the hunt.

Katie Thompson, Mohawk basketweaver, at work.

ONEIDA

"the granite people" or
"the people of the standing stone"

Directly west of the Mohawk, the Iroquois Longhouse sheltered the Oneida, "the granite people" or
"the people of the standing stone."

Over 130 Oneida Indians still live in central New
York. They occupy 350 acres, all that is left of their
ancient tribal lands, which once spread over approximately 6 million acres in upstate New York. Five
million of those acres were sold in 1788 for the tiny sum
of $5,000, plus an annual payment of $600. In 1795 an
additional 300,000 acres were sold at a reported price of
fifty cents an acre.

During the American Revolution the Oneida
fought on the side of the colonists. They proved to be
among the best scouts in the American armies, and
several of their members became high-ranking officers.
On one occasion the Oneida saved the life of the
Marquis de Lafayette, the noted French officer who had
volunteered to help the Americans. The Oneida also
played an important part in defeating the English armies
at Saratoga, which put an end to a grand strategy of
splitting the colonies in two, along the Hudson River.
For their loyalty and bravery, the Oneida earned special
commendation from Gen. George Washington.

After American independence was won, reservation land in New York was retained by the Oneida,
but the Indians lived there for only sixty years. In 1843
they were persuaded to liquidate, or sell, the reservation. Most of the people moved west to Wisconsin,
where new land was bought, a new reservation created,

and new homes built. The Oneida still live on their reservation in Wisconsin.

The 350 acres of the New York reservation that were not sold were divided among the Oneida people who preferred to remain in the East. The land is still considered a reservation by the inhabitants. Other Oneida moved onto a reservation with their Iroquois relatives, the Onondaga, with whom many had intermarried. The enrolled Oneida membership among the Onondaga is about 450. Other Oneida have moved to Iroquois reservations farther west in New York, and some have joined relatives on the Six Nations Reserve in Canada.

When the Oneida gave up their reservation, they also relinquished their rights with the New York State Department on Indian Affairs. They have no rights or privileges different from those held by the New York State population, except their lands are tax exempt. About 20 percent of the Oneida still speak their traditional Iroquois language.

ONONDAGA
"people of the hills"

Almost 1,400 men, women, and children of the Onondaga nation live on a reservation six miles south of Syracuse. The reservation covers 7,300 acres. Before the American Revolution the Onondaga occupied a territory in central New York many times the size of its present home. Much of the tribal land, including the site of present-day Syracuse, was sold early in the 1800s.

The Onondaga, whose name means "people of the hills," are considered the original builders of the Iroquois League. The League was an organization of equals, joined for a common good, and the six Indian nations that made up the League remained independent and free in all matters except defense and war. Even today, when a question has to be decided, the tribal chiefs meet and debate the issue. The meeting takes place around the council fires of the Onondaga, who also supply the leading chief of the Iroquois, the Tado-da-ho, or council tie-breaker, whose function is to keep debate going until total agreement is reached or the matter is dropped.

The meeting place of the Iroquois League council, according to ancient legend, was beneath a towering pine, known as the Evergreen Tree of Peace. On its highest branches an eagle was said to perch, guarding the peace of the people and prepared to warn them of coming dangers.

The council of chiefs of the Iroquois League continues to meet on the Onondaga Reservation. Thus the capital of the modern Six Nation Confederacy is also the Onondaga tribal headquarters.

As "Guardians of the Sacred Council Fires" or "Firekeepers" for the Iroquois League, the Onondaga are responsible for the Indians' wampum belts. Many belts have been put away in the New York State Museum in Albany, but the Onondaga are asking that the wampum be returned to them as sacred and historical objects.

The Onondaga are perhaps the most traditional of the New York State Iroquois. Life on the reservation is organized around the ancient religion of the Longhouse, even though there are several churches of other denominations on the reservation. The Longhouse religion is observed with special services and ceremonials, including the Green Corn Festival. The Onondaga language is still spoken by many of the people.

All people of the Longhouse are eligible to choose a council of fourteen members, who serve the tribe for life.

Although the Onondaga Reservation is located in the fertile bottomland of a dry lake, little agriculture is undertaken. Several stores on the reserve are owned and operated by Indian families.

The children of the tribe go to a school on the reserve from the kindergarten to the sixth grade. For grades seven through twelve the youngsters go off the reserve to a nearby town. Several have gone on to earn college degrees, and some have become university teachers.

The Onondaga believe that their treaty relationships make them a free and independent nation, unaffected by many of the regulations of the state and federal governments. For a long time the tribe has questioned the tax laws of New York and the draft requirements of federal law.

The Onondaga maintain no facilities for non-Indians on their reservation, preferring to treasure the privacy of their homes and heritage.

CAYUGA
"where they land the boats"

The Cayuga Indians, whose name means "where they land the boats," no longer have a reservation in New York. Most Cayuga disposed of their lands and moved to Ohio and later Oklahoma. A few chose to remain with their Iroquois relatives, the Seneca, on the

Seneca's Cattaraugus Reservation, near Buffalo. More than 300 Cayuga people now reside on this reserve and in nearby communities.

The Seneca, whose name means "the people of the big hill," have become divided into two groups in New York.

One group, numbering about 700, is known as the Tonawanda Seneca. About three-fourths of these people live on the Tonawanda Reserve, near the city of Batavia. The rest have left the reservation to make their homes elsewhere in the state or country. The present reserve covers 7,549 acres in Niagara, Erie, and Genessee counties, but before 1857 its extent was 12,000 acres.

For some years it appeared that the Seneca might be forced to move west of the Missouri River, according to a treaty made twenty years earlier by the Indians and the United States government. The treaty was denounced by the Tonawanda section of the tribe, which split from the rest of the Seneca. In 1857 the Tonawanda group sold the western lands that they had been assigned and bought their present holdings within their traditional homeland.

The split among the Seneca was caused primarily by differences in religious affiliation. While other Seneca accepted the teachings of Christian missionaries, the Tonawanda group held to their traditional Iroquois faith. They had become followers of a chief called

Wearing traditional headgear, Cayuga chief Howard Skye beats Iroquois water drum.

Handsome Lake, who lived during the time of the American Revolution.

Handsome Lake had brooded silently for many years over the tragic fate of his fellow Indians. He saw them being driven from their homes, wracked by strange diseases, and ruined by alcohol. Eventually he emerged from his despair and came out among his people, urging them to take heart, to preserve their traditions and give up evil ways. The "Good Message" of Handsome Lake was accepted by many of the Seneca, as well as other Iroquois people. It is still the fundamental faith of the Longhouse religion, and the Seneca have become "Keepers of the Good Faith."

The Tonawanda people conduct their religious and social activities in and around a modern community building on their reserve. Ceremonial dances are held several times during the year, and the traditional sport of lacrosse is played against both Indian and non-Indian teams.

The tribe is governed under a New York Indian law written by a Tonawanda Seneca, Eli S. Parker, who was Commissioner of Indian Affairs under President Ulysses S. Grant. Every year the Tonawanda Seneca elect a president, clerk, treasurer, marshall, and three peacemakers. Male Indians of full age, whose names are on the tribal rolls, are eligible to vote. As in ancient days, the clan mothers elect the clan chiefs, who serve for life or until they fail to fulfill their office. The chiefs constitute a council for the tribe.

The Tonawanda Seneca have no tribal income. No commercial or industrial establishments are located on their reservation. The people work on farms and in mills, factories, and other businesses in the nearby towns and cities.

The children of the tribe attend schools in these same communities. Vocational training is offered in the community building, and the tribe has scholarship funds available for deserving students, some of whom have gone on to college.

The deed for the Tonawanda Reservation was taken out in trust in the name of the United States Secretary of the Interior, who conveyed the land to the comptroller of the state of New York, also in trust for the Indians. The land was allotted to the members of the tribe, who are governed by federal regulations if they lease or mortgage their holdings. The land cannot be disposed of without the permission of the Secretary of the Interior.

The second group of Seneca includes the major portion of the tribe. These people gave up their traditional Indian government, and many were converted to Christianity. Later they joined together and formed the Seneca Nation of Indians.

"The Eagle Dance," painting by Tonawanda Seneca artist Ernest Smith.

Three reservations serve the Seneca Nation. One, the Oil Springs Reserve at Cuba Lake in southwestern New York, is uninhabited. The larger of the other two is the Allegany Reservation, near the New York-Pennsylvania border. Of its 30,469 tribally owned acres, 10,000 acres are leased to the villages of Kill Buck, Vandalia, Carrolltown, and Salamanca. The reservation's Seneca population is approximately 1,200; non-Indian residents total nearly 8,500.

Along the shores of Lake Erie, south of the city of Buffalo, is the Seneca Nation's Cattaraugus Reservation, extending over 21,680 acres in three counties. This land also is tribally owned. The Indian population is about 2,400, twice that of the Allegany Reservation. Both reserves also house Cayuga and Onondaga Indians, who have moved in with their Iroquois relatives.

The boundaries of the Allegany and Cattaraugus reservations were established in 1794 by a treaty that provides the tribe with an annual payment of cloth and a small amount of cash. The land is vested in the Seneca Nation and cannot be sold without the consent of the United States government. Individual Seneca Indians are assigned the right to use or cultivate the land.

Since the reservations were created, they have lost an estimated 2,000 acres to gas and electric power lines, highways, and railroads. Even more has been lost to a giant dam.

Twenty miles downstream in the Allegheny River, which flows through the Allegany Reservation, the huge Kinzua Dam has been built. Its name is derived from an Iroquois word meaning "a fish on a spear." The dam was constructed to provide flood control and electric power for cities along the river some miles away.

When the Kinzua Dam was finished, the waters of the river backed up, creating a lake thirty-five miles long that destroyed many Seneca homes and covered approximately 10,000 acres of reservation land. The Indians were resettled in modest, modern homes, which were financed out of the $12 million paid to the Seneca Nation for the land flooded by the dam. The nation also used the money to build two community houses, one on each reserve, and invested the rest for building and educational purposes. Scholarships for higher education were made available to young people of the tribe.

The tribal headquarters of the Seneca Nation is in Irving, which is located on the Cattaraugus Reservation. The nation has undertaken to manage the internal affairs of its people on both reservations, although since 1784 the Indians' health, education, welfare, and legal services have been the responsibility of the state of New York, which also exercises civil and criminal jurisdiction over the area.

In 1884 the Seneca Nation adopted a constitution that did away with the traditional chiefs. Instead

Effie C. Johnson, Seneca grandmother, shows young Sharon Bova the empty darkness over Kinzua Dam.

executive, legislative, and judicial branches of government were established. A tribal council of sixteen members, eight from each reservation, now handles the affairs of the people.

Both male and female members of the Seneca Nation, when they are twenty-one years of age, may vote in tribal elections and hold office. However, following Iroquois tradition, membership in the tribe descends through the line of the mother, not the father, and only children of female members can inherit or acquire the land allotments or rights available to the tribe.

Although the Seneca Nation manages its own affairs through its tribal leaders, it can call upon an agent of the Bureau of Indian Affairs, a division of the United States Department of the Interior, for consultation and advice.

For several years both Seneca Nation reserves enjoyed a sizable annual income from the sale of sand and gravel for highway construction, but that source of revenue is coming to an end as road building is completed. On the Allegany Reservation the major employment center is the city of Salamanca, which has two furniture factories, two railroad shops, a plastics manufacturer, a lumber mill, milling and electronic plants, and numerous wholesale and retail businesses. The Cattaraugus Reservation boasts several small manufacturing plants in its Seneca Nation Industrial Park, which has the advantage of being close to the big-city facilities of Buffalo.

The Seneca Nation also has plans for other tribal business enterprises that can provide income for the people. Among the plans are sports and recreational facilities, one tentatively called Seneca Overlook, which is to be a recreational area along the Allegheny Reservoir. Other plans call for building an educational and recreational complex named Iroquoia, which will include a 200-room motel, a museum for Iroquois artifacts, a sports field, a 1,100-seat amphitheater, and three Indian villages.

Education for the Seneca children on the Cattaraugus Reservation is supplied by elementary and secondary schools in nearby communities. Children on the Allegany Reservation attend public or parochial schools in Salamanca.

TUSCARORA
"the weavers of the cloth" or
"the shirt-wearing people"

The Five Nations of the Iroquois became the Six Nations early in the eighteenth century when they were joined by the Tuscarora. The Tuscarora were of kindred Iroquois stock, but they had lived in North Carolina where they had learned new ways. Their cultural difference from the New York Iroquois is reflected in their name, which means "the weavers of the cloth" or "the shirt-wearing people."

Struggles with the colonists had broken up the Tuscarora tribe in North Carolina. Some had fled farther south. Others had stayed nearby, hidden in the hills. Still others had struggled wearily northward, reaching New Jersey and New York where they were adopted into the Iroquois Confederacy in 1718.

The Tuscarora Reservation is located nine miles northeast of the city of Niagara Falls. It extends over 5,700 acres. Part of the land was a gift from the Seneca; the rest was purchased from a land company with the money received from the sale of the tribe's North Carolina holdings. In recent years 550 acres of the Tuscarora reservation were taken by the New York State Power Authority for use as a reservoir. Approximately $850,000 was given to the tribe as payment.

The Tuscarora today number around 650 people. They are governed by a council made up of the chiefs and headmen of the tribe. The reservation is collectively owned by the whole nation, and the council governs the use of the land and its natural resources. An individual only rents a portion, which is allotted to him by the council. He has the right to sell for his own benefit only the timber he clears away to make room for cultivation.

The Indians engage in both farming and small business on the reservation. One farming cooperative, several trailer camps, car-wrecking yards, auto repair garages, a grocery store, and a soda fountain are in operation.

Life for the Tuscarora has elements of both the traditional and the modern. Generally they live in much the same way as any other back-country community. Their children are encouraged to continue their education. Most go to schools in nearby communities. Added educational facilities are available in the tribe's school and Council House. Some of the Tuscarora still speak their ancient language, and the tribe, like most Iroquois, still determines its membership through the female line. Only the children of a Tuscarora mother are eligible to share in the tribe's resources. The oldest mother in each of the nine clans also chooses the clan chief. The chiefs hold their office for a lifetime, but can be removed for misbehavior.

Ancient treaties are still in force between New York and several of the Iroquois tribes. Under their terms the following payments are made each year: Cayuga, $2,300; Onondaga, $2,430; St. Regis Mohawks, $2,132; Seneca, $500. In addition, the Cayuga receive an annual interest payment from the $433,447 paid for land sales before 1800. The Onondaga also are the recipients yearly of 150 bushels of salt.

The United States government makes certain other payments to the New York Iroquois in accordance with other treaties and agreements. Cloth, worth $4,500, is distributed annually to all of the Six Nations with the exception of the St. Regis Mohawks. A yearly sum of $16,250 is paid to the Seneca, representing the interest on funds held in trust for them by the federal treasury.

In addition to the Iroquois, New York is the home of a small number of Algonquian-speaking people, most of whom live east of the Hudson River and on Long Island.

SHINNECOCK
"at the level land"

The larger of the two Long Island reservations is the home of the Shinnecock Indians. Located along the south shore near Southampton, the reserve covers 400 acres, left to the Indians by the king of England in colonial days. The land, in one of the most valuable areas near New York City, is valued at more than $100,000 per acre.

The Shinnecock population on the reserve numbers around 200. None can speak the Algonquian language of their forefathers, though the meaning of their tribal name is known to be "at the level land."

The early Shinnecock, once part of the Montauk Confederacy on Long Island, were expert fishermen and whalers. Little of their seagoing heritage remains among modern Shinnecock men who make their living in the surrounding communities.

The tribe, under the supervision of the state of New York, is governed by an elected body of three land trustees, one of whom acts as tribal president, a second as secretary, and the third as treasurer.

The second Algonquian reservation on Long Island is the home of the Poospatuck, or Patchoag, Indians.

POOSPATUCK or PATCHOAG
"where a creek
bursts forth, flows out"

The Poospatuck Reservation covers sixty acres near Riverhead, ten miles away, and Brookhaven, five miles away. About 85 Indians maintain homes on the reserve. They are governed by their elected land trustees, who also serve as president, secretary, and treasurer of the tribe.

The reservation dates to pre-Revolutionary War days, when it was established by the government on behalf of the king of England. The Poospatuck, also whalers and fishermen, were related tribally to the Indians of Connecticut, across Long Island Sound. Their name means "where a creek bursts forth."

MONTAUK
"at the fort"

Less than fifty members of a third Algonquian tribe, the Montauk, still live at the eastern end of Long Island, near the point to which they have given their name. The language of the Montauk Indians has been forgotten. Their name, thought to reflect their need for military protection, has been translated to mean "at the fort." The tribe does not live on reservation land and has no special governing bodies.

A few other Algonquian groups live along the Hudson River and in the foothills of the Adirondack Mountains. They do not occupy reservation land nor

Poospatuck Indian spearing eels at mouth of Mystic Creek, Long Island.

██

ABNAKI or WABANAKI
"people of the sunrise"

██

receive special services from the state or federal governments. Near Lake George is a community of about
twenty-five Abnakis, or Wabanakis, the "people of the
sunrise," who at one time lived in New England. A few
of these Algonquians still speak their native language.

Two groups of social isolates live within the
boundaries of New York State. Neither group has
proven Indian origins. They do not live on reservations
nor receive special services. One group is known as the
Bushwackers, or Pondshiners, and numbers around
100, according to a recent count. The other group totals
almost 500 people called Jackson Whites. The Jackson
Whites also live in New Jersey.

NEW JERSEY

New Jersey is the home of about 4,700 Indians, an increase of almost 3,000 persons in ten years. The current figure is twenty times the state's Indian population in 1930 and about 800 times the 1900 figure.

The Indians in the state are members of several tribes. They do not have any organized reserves or settlements. About 85 percent of them live in urban centers.

New Jersey is still the home of some Delaware Indians, who were the native people of the area. The Indians' name for themselves was *Lenni Lenape*, which means "true men." They were given the name *Delaware* after Lord De La Warr, the seventeenth-century English governor of the territory.

▀▀▀

LENNI LENAPE

"true men"

▀▀▀

The Lenni Lenape were members of the Algonquian Delaware Confederacy, which occupied the basin of the Delaware River in eastern Pennsylvania, southeastern New York, most of New Jersey, and all of Delaware. Indians of the Delaware Confederacy were the ones who first encountered the Dutch and Swedish settlers. They also met with William Penn in 1662.

Early in the eighteenth century the Delaware Confederacy came under the domination of the Iroquois of New York. The Algonquians then found themselves being pushed out of their homelands by increasing settlements and forced to move west. Most moved to present-day Oklahoma, some found their way as far as Texas, and a few remained in New Jersey.

In the middle of the eighteenth century Tuscarora Indians, driven out of North Carolina, reached New Jersey on the way to their Iroquois kinsmen in New York. Some of the Tuscarora remained in New Jersey.

Later, members of another tribe, the Cherokee, also settled in the state. They lived among the Lenni Lenape, and the two tribes intermarried.

Every year in the early summer the Indians of New Jersey become hosts to visitors from many parts of the United States who gather for the Monroe Powwow at East Brunswick. Indians and non-Indians come together then to display their skills in tribal dancing, singing, and handicrafts, such as basketmaking and beadwork.

The Monroe Powwow represents a mixture of people, very much like Americans everywhere throughout the country. The Indians are often indistinguishable

Lenni Lenape Indian, wearing tribal dress. The New Jersey Indians were often called Delawares.

from their non-Indian admirers. Most New Jersey Indians now speak the same language, attend the same schools, and work at similar jobs as non-Indians. At the same time, traditional tribal ceremonies, ancient nature lore, and craft work attract many non-Indian Americans.

New Jersey's population also includes several groups of people whose historical origins and identities are still mysteries. According to population counts almost twenty-five years old, about 800 Jackson Whites and nearly 500 persons called Pineys reside in the state. Another group, named Gouldtown, has an undetermined number of members.

PENNSYLVANIA

There are no longer any officially recognized Indian groups or Indian communities in Pennsylvania. However, over 5,500 Indians from many tribes still reside in the state, scattered throughout the cities and countryside. This 1970 census figure represents more than a twofold increase since 1960 and a tenfold increase since 1930.

At one time Pennsylvania did have a 600-acre Indian reserve, called the Cornplanter Grant. It was a section of a land grant made to the Seneca chief, Cornplanter, just after the American Revolution. The Cornplanter Grant is now under the waters of the Allegheny River, which was backed up by the Kinzua Dam.

POOLE
shortening of Vanderpoole

About 500 people whose origins are listed as either "Indian remnant groups" or "unknown Indian identity" still live in northern Pennsylvania. They are known as the Pooles, and their homes at South Towanda and Wyalusing are generally called Pooletown, which some scholars describe as a "submerged Indian community."

The Pooles' beginnings in Pennsylvania have been traced to 1792, when four Indian men emerged from the forest of nearby New York and found work as hunters with some Pennsylvania settlers. Soon afterwards the men were joined by their wives and later by other Indians. The Pooles received their name, it is believed, from a man named Anthony Vanderpoole, a descendant of the Mohawk Indians of New York.

In the early seventeenth century, when the Dutch were settling in New York, the Pooles changed their language from Mohawk to Dutch. In less than 200 years, after the British took over New York, the Pooles made another language switch from Dutch to English. Today some older Pooles still speak a unique dialect of the English language. Their speech is rapid, rather high-pitched and musical, and usually unintelligible to their non-Indian neighbors. The Poole speech style is dying out, however, because of the more accepted language habits taught in the local schools.

The Poole family structure also seems unique. It appears to be patterned after the Iroquois, but with variations. Children are taught the customs and manners of their people not only by their parents, but, more

Edward Hicks painted many versions of the scene which he imagined:
William Penn and the treaty with the Indians of Pennsylvania.

Kinzua Dam, backing up the waters of the Allegheny River which
flooded part of the Seneca reserve in New York and Pennsylvania.

importantly, by the example of other children of their own age.

The Pooles do not have any political structures peculiarly their own.

They live by small-scale farming and by hunting, woodcutting, and food gathering in the forest. They also hire out as day laborers on neighboring non-Indian farms. Their own farmsteads are quite small. The soil is tended in typical Indian fashion; the earth is not plowed, but is turned with a spade to prepare it for planting. The crops are mixed. Hogs and chickens are the most common domesticated animals.

Members of the newer generation of Pooles are being trained for work away from the farms. Many have become skilled mechanics, machinists, patternmakers, and diemakers. Equipped with new skills, the younger Pooles have tended to drift away from their northern Pennsylvania birthplace in search of greater job opportunities elsewhere. A strong group feeling continues, however, impelling them to return often.

A small band of about 100 persons in Pennsylvania has a different claim to an Indian identity. These people live in the mountains near Harrisburg and are said to be Indians of Cherokee descent. The group has no special Indian territory, enjoys no particular privileges, and speaks no Indian language. Some scholars dispute their "Indianness" and think they are better considered a mountaineer group.

DELAWARE

Two-thirds of Delaware's nearly 700 Indians still live in the rural areas of the state, rather than in the towns and cities. The state's Indian population has not altered much in the past ten years, the increase being less than 10 percent. Years ago, however, the Delaware Indians were probably not carefully counted when the census was taken. In 1930 their number was listed as five, and in 1900 it was nine.

The Nanticoke tribe accounts for about 200 of the state's Indians. The Nanticoke are members of the Algonquian language family. Their name means "tide-water people," indicating their early location along the rivers and coast.

NANTICOKE
"tidewater people"

The early English settlers of Delaware crowded most of the Nanticoke out of their homes along the Nanticoke River. In 1722 the Indians began to abandon their villages and move northward. For a while they settled along the Susquehanna River in northern Pennsylvania and southern New York. Later they moved again, different groups traveling to Canada, Ohio, and Indiana. Nanticoke Indians still live among the Iroquois on the Six Nations Reserve in Ontario, Canada.

Other Nanticoke, descendants of the Indians who refused to move from Delaware, live along the Indian River, near the river's mouth on the Atlantic Ocean. They are mostly farmers and fishermen. They live in a close community, but their language has been forgotten, and their tribal dress and ceremonials have disappeared.

Before 1962 the Nanticoke had their own school, but since that time the children have attended public schools in nearby Millsboro. One traditional group ceremony is still held every year in October. It is the annual homecoming when as many as 200 Nanticoke assemble at the Indian Mission Church for an all-day program and dinner. Except for this one event, the lives of the Nanticoke are very much like the lives of their non-Indian rural neighbors.

A group of people of probable Indian descent also resides in Delaware. Known as the Moors, they number over 300.

According to tradition, they are descended from a crew of Moorish sailors who were shipwrecked near the

Charles Cullen Clark, chief of the Nanticoke Indians, wearing eagle feather headdress.

outlet of the Indian River. The sailors escaped to the Delaware shore and intermarried with the Indians living there. There are variations of the story, one of which lists the early Moors as pirates from the Spanish Main.

The Moors speak no Indian language, have no reservation land, and enjoy no special government services.

MARYLAND

At the beginning of the twentieth century the number of Indians in Maryland was registered as three. The census of 1930 listed a total of fifty. The influx of Indians from the South during World War II brought Maryland's 1960 total to almost 1,600, a figure that more than doubled to 4,239 in 1970. Over 85 percent of the Indians in Maryland live in the state's urban communities.

Several thousand Indians from North Carolina make their homes, more or less permanently, in Baltimore. These people are the Lumbee Indians, who came north to find employment in the city's factories and commercial establishments.

WESORTS
derived from "we sort of people"

Maryland's original inhabitants, the Nanticoke, still have a few descendants in the Blue Ridge Mountain areas. A fairly large group of people of probable Indian heritage, called the Wesorts, live in the swamplands in the southern part of the state. There are two versions of the origin of the name *Wesort.* It may be a corruption of the word *wisoes,* meaning "elders of the council," or a shortened form of the phrase "we sort of people." The *Wesorts* are supposed to be descended from the Piscataway or Conoy Indians, who first settled along the Kanawha (Conoy) River.

The Indians of Maryland have no special status. They speak no separate language, have no special land privileges, and work at jobs on the farms and in the cities, just as the general population does. Indian children attend school with everyone else.

The state maintains no distinct supervisory agency for the Indian population.

WASHINGTON, D.C.

No official Indian territory exists within the capital city of Washington, D.C.

After 1634 some Conoy Indians, an Algonquian people related to both the Nanticoke of Delaware and Maryland and to the Powhatan of Virginia, found homes along the Potomac River, probably near the site of present-day Washington. The Conoys, who were also known as the Piscataway Indians, remained along the Potomac for a very few years. In 1675 they were driven away by the pressure of tribes from the North and of settlers from the Virginia colonies. Within a century their numbers had been reduced to about 150. Eventually they left the area entirely and became submerged among the Delaware and Mahican tribes.

CONOY or PISCATAWAY
derived from Kanawha River

According to the 1970 census, 956 American Indians from all over the United States live in Washington, D.C. This represents a growth of 60 percent in the ten years since 1960. In 1940 only forty Indians lived in the capital, and in 1900 there were only twenty-two.

VIRGINIA

According to the 1970 census, nearly 5,000 Indians live in Virginia. Only a portion of this total belongs to the four historic tribes of the state: the Pamunkey, the Mattaponi, the Chickahominy, and the Rappahannock. All of these tribes are of Algonquian stock, but they no longer speak their native tongues.

The Indians of Virginia were among the first to encounter the English settlers of America. At the time the tribes were joined in an alliance called the Powhatan Confederacy. The settlers mistakenly applied the name of the entire alliance to the chief of the Confederacy, who became known in history as Chief Powhatan.

One of the largest tribes of the Powhatan Confederacy was the Pamunkey, who numbered well over 1,000.

PAMUNKEY
"sloping hill"

Their tribal name means "sloping hill." During the early colonization of Virginia the Pamunkey captured Captain John Smith, the chief military figure in the English settlement. Smith would have been beheaded had he not been saved at the last minute by the pleas of Pocahontas, daughter of Chief Powhatan.

Old woodcut shows Captain John Smith capturing Pamunkey chief.

Pocahontas, daughter of Powhatan chief, painted in London.

King Powhatan comands C: Smith to be slayne, his daughter Pokahontas beggs his life his thankfulness and how he subieted 39 of their kings. reade history.

Old woodcut shows Pocahontas begging her father to spare Captain John Smith.

The Indians' friendship with the Virginia colonists did not last long after the death of Chief Powhatan. Powhatan's younger brother, Opechancanough, tried for twenty years to drive the English out of Virginia, leading his men in two desperate wars, which finally ended in 1646. The peace terms created reservations for the Pamunkey and the Mattaponi and exacted tokens of tribute from the Indians. The tribute was a brace of wild duck or geese or a deer to be paid to the governor of Virginia every year at Thanksgiving. The gift is no longer compulsory, but the Indians continue the tradition each autumn.

The Pamunkey Reserve covers about 800 acres along the Pamunkey River, a few miles northeast of the state capital, Richmond. The Indian land is low and marshy, dotted with wooded patches. Only half of the land can be used for farming. A permanent population of forty lives on the reservation, according to a recent census.

Special license plates on Pamunkey Indian car.

Ploughed fields and an Indian home on the Pamunkey reservation, Virginia.

The Pamunkey are governed by a chief and a council of five men, who are elected every four years. At one time the chief served for life. The tribe has a unique way of electing its officials. On election night each Pamunkey man who is eligible to vote is given a kernel of corn and a pea. A vote for a candidate is marked by dropping the corn into the ballot box. The pea represents a vote against him.

The Pamunkey tribal organization has been democratic since the establishment of the reservation in 1646. The people pay no personal or property taxes, but are subject to other kinds of assessments. The state of Virginia, which supervises the reserve, provides no aid except the maintenance of a day school. The Indians themselves support a Baptist church on the reservation.

Indian home on Pamunkey Reserve, on banks of Pamunkey River.

The Pamunkey continue an ancient tradition as hunters and fishermen. They often work as guides for hunting and fishing parties in their area. An important commercial fish is shad, which the Indians catch in the Pamunkey River.

The Pamunkey were among the first Indians east of the Mississippi River to make a true form of fired pottery. The women still work actively as potters, making use of the native clay to fashion pitchers, bowls, and plates. Other handicrafts still being practiced are beadwork, leatherwork, belt-making, and the manufacture of moccasins, feathered headdresses, dolls, and miniature drums, or tom-toms.

MATTAPONI
"bad bread" or "no bread at all"

There are approximately 200 Mattaponi and Upper Mattaponi Indians in Virginia. The Upper Mattaponi do not live on special Indian land, but about 50 Mattaponi have homes on a reservation near Richmond, in King William County. The reservation extends over 125 acres and is held in trust for the Indians by the state of Virginia.

The Mattaponi on the reservation use it for farming or other personal purposes. They have lifetime rights to their holdings, but they cannot sell the land either to another member of the tribe or to a nonmember. The reserve is circled by a strip of forestland, largely owned by the Indians. Unlike the reservation property, the forest area can be bought and sold.

The Mattaponi on the reservation still live under their own form of government as they did years ago. They elect their own chief and council. Some of the men work in the lumber industry in nearby forests. The children attend local public schools. An effort to keep alive their own history and tradition is shown in a tribal museum on the reservation. Among the relics preserved are stone weapons reported to have been used in the wars against the English.

The name *Mattaponi* means "no bread at all."

Chickahominy Indian school at Samaria, Virginia.

CHICKAHOMINY
"hominy" or
"coarse-pounded corn" people

The Chickahominy Indians of Virginia number around 650. Their name means "hominy" or "course-pounded corn" people.

The Chickahominy occupy an area of approximately 2,000 acres in New Kent and Charles City counties, not far from Richmond. Their homeland is not a reservation. The Indians own the land as individuals, not as a tribe. Their individual holdings vary in size, some being as small as a single acre and others covering

Church building, Chickahominy Indian community, Virginia.

as many as 200 acres. The Chickahominy may sell their property, but only to another Indian and only under certain conditions.

Because their land is not classified as a reservation, the Chickahominy have the same rights and obligations as other Virginia citizens to pay taxes and to vote in state and federal elections. In spite of their status as full citizens of the state, however, the Chickahominy still maintain forms of self-government. Every four years they choose a council of four members and the tribal officers of chief, assistant chief, secretary, and recording secretary.

When they were first encountered by Europeans, the Chickahominy were governed by a chief and a council of great men, called mangai. The tribe was allied to the other tribes of the Powhatan Confederacy, but it managed to maintain itself as an independent group at all times. The tribal land was between the Chickahominy and the Pamunkey rivers.

Within forty years, however, the Indian way of life was undermined by the Virginia colonists. The Chickahominy joined the Powhatan Confederacy and Chief Opechancanough in the wars against the settlers, but the struggle was hopeless. The Indian defeat cost the Chickahominy most of their homeland, then an area of about 6,000 acres.

For a century afterward Virginia Indians were people in distress. Their own world had been destroyed, and they could find no place in the mushrooming non-Indian society. The Chickahominy tribe grew smaller and smaller. Many of the tribespeople left Virginia to search for new homes in the North. Some went as far north as Canada, seeking a stronger tribe that would take them in.

During the last half of the 1800s the Chickahominy were finally able to find a place for themselves in Virginia. Near Providence Forge, not far from Richmond, they took over an empty church building, called the Samaria Baptist Church, in which they established a school for their children. Once almost exclusively for Indian children, the school has now been included in the state system and is attended by many non-Indians. Also, the school's teaching staff is no longer all Indian.

With the school as a start, the Chickahominy were able to recreate their own community, where they still reside. They live and work as do most other isolated rural people in Virginia. Many Chickahominy young people have gone on with their education and become doctors, engineers, teachers, and office workers. At the same time, the tribe has tried to preserve the traditional ways of its Indian past.

RAPPAHANNOCK
"people of the ebb-and-flow stream"

Two hundred members of the Rappahannock tribe still live in Virginia, while several hundred others reside elsewhere in the United States. The Virginia Rappahannock live mostly in King and Queen, Caroline, and Essex counties, as part of the general rural population.

The Rappahannock are the descendants of several Powhatan tribal groups, which were driven out of their homes during the Virginia colonial wars. Remnants of the ancient Rappahannocks and others, like the northern Nansemond, merged with part of the Mattaponi and Piscataway to form a new Indian community. The name *Rappahannock* means "people of the ebb and flow stream."

The modern Rappahannock tribe was reorganized in 1921, when it was granted a charter by the state, and tribal officers were elected. The tribe's membership at the time totaled about 350.

Many problems faced the Rappahannock, primarily in employment, civil rights, and education for their children. At first the children were taught in private homes. Later King and Queen County hired an Indian teacher to teach the elementary grades in a one-room schoolhouse. In more recent years Rappahannock children have been enrolled in the public school system.

Other groups of people identified as Indians are scattered throughout Virginia. In the Piedmont and Blue Ridge mountains there are several hundred Potomacs and smaller bands of Accohanoes and Nansemonds. Also in the area are groups, known as the Brown People and the "Amherst County issues," who are probably Indians though their origins are not known. Indian ancestry is also claimed by a people in Patrick County and a large group, known as Melungeons, or Ramps, who live in the steep, almost inaccessible heights of the Appalachian Mountains, which spill into Tennessee and Kentucky.

The Melungeons are a distinct group of people, who have intermarried for years. They have dark complexions, high cheekbones, and straight to wavy hair, indicating a racial mixture of Indian, white, and black. The people think of themselves as having Portuguese ancestry, which is one explanation for their name, which may have come from the Portuguese word *melungo*, meaning "shipwrecked." Other explanations are that their name is derived from the French word *melange*, meaning "mixture," or the Greek word *melan*, meaning "colored." The Melungeons, or Ramps, live by small-scale farming and root gathering.

The Indian population of Virginia more than doubled in the ten years between 1960 and 1970, when 4,853 were recorded. The increase has been sixfold since 1930 and almost fifteenfold since 1900.

NORTH CAROLINA

With over 44,000 Indians living within its borders, North Carolina has the largest population of Native Americans of any state on the Atlantic seaboard. The census shows an increase of over 6,000 Indians in the ten years between 1960 and 1970. The current total is nearly three times the 1930 figure and eight times the 1900 figure.

The five major Indian groups in North Carolina are the Haliwa; the Lumbee; the Eastern, or Qualla, Cherokee; the Waccamaw; and the Coharie. Recent statistics list 3,000 Coharie Indians in Sampson and adjoining counties.

The historical origins of all North Carolina Indians are not totally clear. Those who identify themselves as

Indians include about 4,000 people called Smilings; approximately 300 people called Cubans, who also live in Virginia; and about 2,000 persons who belong to several groupings in Rockingham, Stokes, and Surry counties.

The North Carolina Indians who call themselves the Haliwa number approximately 2,000. They live near the northern border of the state, close to the headwaters of the Roanoke River.

HALIWA
modern name formed by combining
Halifax and Warren counties

The name of *Haliwa* is not derived from any Indian tongue. It is the combination of the names of the two counties in which the tribe lives: *Hali* (from Halifax) and *wa* (from Warren). *Haliwa* became the official name of the people by an act of the North Carolina legislature in 1965. At that time the tribal organization was also established, with officers consisting of a chief, vice chief, secretary, treasurer, and a council.

The Haliwa live just like the other residents of Halifax and Warren counties. They work as businessmen, professionals, and laborers on the farms and in the industries nearby. The Haliwa no longer speak a native language. Their children are enrolled in the regular school system.

The Haliwa trace their Indian ancestry to the Iroquois-speaking Tuscarora Indians, whose homelands were in Halifax and Warren counties several hundred years ago. Early in the 1700s the English settlers in North Carolina sought to expand beyond the seacoast into the interior, only to find the Indians in their path.

In the warfare that broke out, the Tuscarora were defeated and almost completely driven away.

Most of the Indians who were able fled northward, finally joining their kinsmen as the Sixth Nation of the Iroquois in New York. Other tribesmen, who were wounded or sick and unable to make the long journey, found hiding places in the hills of North Carolina and remained. The modern Haliwa claim descent from these survivors. A few of the Tuscarora fled south and lost their identity among the Cherokee Indians in Cumberland County, near the South Carolina border. Some of these people are now trying to retrace their historical lineage.

LUMBEE
"black water"

North Carolina's Robeson County, located in the southern part of the state in the valley of the Lumber, once the Lumbee, River, is the home of approximately 32,000 American Indians, called the Lumbee. They are the largest tribal group on the Atlantic seaboard, and they make up one-third of the Robeson County population. The Lumbee's educational and cultural center is the town of Pembroke, the seat of what was once the tribe's own college.

The Lumbee trace their origin to the earliest colony attempted by the English on American soil. It was established in 1584 on Roanoke Island off the Carolina coast by Sir Walter Raleigh. The colony's governor was John White, who later returned to England for several years. When Governor White finally sailed back to Roanoke Island, the colony had disappeared. All that he could find were some buried possessions and a scrawled message that seemed to indicate that the colonists had gone off with some Indians to a place named Croaton. White considered the remnants left behind by the English colonists to be a "token of their safe being." The Roanoke colony has come to be known as the Lost Colony.

The Lumbee who believe that they are the descendants of the Lost Colony point out that many of the tribespeople have the same names as the sixteenth-century settlers. The Lumbee have borne these names ever since the earliest known records. In addition, although many of the Lumbee are typically Indian in skin coloring and hair texture, others are blue-eyed and blond-haired.

Officially, the Lumbee claim of descent from the Lost Colony is not accepted. Three other possible origins are that the Lumbee are descended from the Cherokee, the Tuscarora, or the eastern Siouan-speaking Catawba, who live across the state's border in South Carolina.

The Lumbee first came to public attention during the middle years of the eighteenth century. They were living on and farming the areas that they still occupy. Their speech was English, and many were slaveholders, just as their neighboring non-Indian plantation owners were.

Since that time the Lumbee have borne a succession of names: Croatan Indians, Indians of Robeson County, and Cherokee Indians of Robeson County. In 1956 the people were given the Lumbee name by which they are now known.

During the early years of World War II many Lumbee people left their traditional homeland and went north to take advantage of the employment opportunities in the large cities. More than 3,500 settled in Baltimore, Maryland, where they still occupy a section in the center of the city. In Baltimore they became teachers, social workers, carpenters, painters, as well as factory hands and office personnel. But the Baltimore tribe members retain their ties with their kinsmen in North Carolina and frequently return to visit.

The Lumbee of North Carolina have no special privileges as Indians. They share the responsibilities of citizenship with their neighbors, both black and white. They speak no distinct Indian language and no longer operate any schools completely their own. Through the years the Lumbee have established themselves in the general economic community. Some are owners of sizable tracts of land in Robeson County. Others have filled a variety of jobs, from farmhand to college president.

CHEROKEE
"people of a different tongue"

Approximately 5,000 members of the Eastern Band of the Cherokee live high up in the Great Smoky Mountains, near the western tip of North Carolina. They live on one of the few reservations in the East that is under the supervision of the federal, rather than a state, government. The Bureau of Indian Affairs, a division of the United States Department of the Interior in Washington, D.C., directly oversees the Cherokee Reservation in North Carolina.

Sprawling over 56,400 acres of mountains and forests, the Eastern Cherokee reserve has three major

Headquarters of Cherokee Nation, emblazoned with tribal seal.

sections. The main area, called the Qualla Boundary, covers almost three-fourths of the total territory and includes the community of Cherokee, North Carolina, seat of the tribal government. Another 3,000 acres nearby is known as the Thomas Tract. The remainder of the land is divided into smaller reservation areas in a region of national forest.

The meaning of the name *Cherokee* is uncertain. It may have stemmed from an Indian word applied to the Cherokee when they first appeared in the eastern states. The word was *Tciloki* or *Tsalagi*, mispronounced "Cherokee." It meant "people of a different tongue." The Cherokee name for themselves was *Ani Yunwiya*, which means "real people."

The Cherokee are members of the Iroquois language family, related to the Iroquois of central New York. Their language was indeed different from that of other North Carolina Indians, who spoke an Algonquian language in the north and a Siouan tongue in the south.

When the first Europeans began to arrive, the Cherokee nation was spread across the territories of six states: North and South Carolina, Virginia, Tennessee, Georgia, and Alabama. The Indians were an energetic people, who had already become farmers as well as hunters and fishermen. They had developed handicrafts, which included colorful masks, pottery, and a variety of woven baskets.

Cherokee territory, rich and fertile, was eyed eagerly by land-hungry settlers. Soon antagonisms between the colonists and the Indians broke into open warfare. The Cherokee lost heavily in these conflicts and found themselves forced off more and more of their land. Their crops were destroyed and their lives constantly threatened.

During the American Revolution the Cherokee supported the English rather than the American colonists. After the defeat of the English the Cherokee continued to occupy 43,000 square miles of land. Included was all of the land in the present-day reservation.

Within a few years, during the War of 1812, the Cherokee shifted their allegiance and fought for the Americans against the British. After the war the tribe was eager to remain on friendly terms with their new allies. In 1827 the Cherokee Nation was organized, modeled after the republican form of government of the United States. A constitution and a new code of laws were adopted. The Cherokee government consisted of a legislature of thirty-two members and a chief with executive powers. The capital of the new Cherokee Nation was established in Georgia.

The Cherokee seemed determined to transform themselves into a model nation of the early nineteenth century. One Cherokee named Sequoya, who could

Goliath George teaching children the alphabet of the Cherokee language at a school near the Cherokee Reservation.

neither read nor write, spent twelve years perfecting a "talking leaf," as he called the first alphabet ever devised for an Indian language. Sequoya's syllabary consisted of eighty-five symbols, representing all the sounds in the Cherokees' spoken language. In a short time the people of the tribe had learned to read and write their language. The first newspaper in an Indian tongue was published by the Cherokee.

The Cherokee language is still spoken by many adult members of the tribe, and it continues to be

Horse Dance, traditional ceremony at Cherokee Reservation, North Carolina.

taught to the Indian children. The proceedings of the Cherokee tribal government are recorded in both Cherokee and English, both of which are in general use on the reservation.

All of the efforts of the Cherokee to modernize their affairs, however, were to no avail. There was no way that an independent, self-governing Indian nation could maintain itself within the political framework of the eastern states. Georgia, in particular, would not tolerate a separate political presence inside its borders.

In 1838–39, despite decisions of the United States Supreme Court and all the efforts of the tribe, the Cherokee were ordered to abandon their homes and to move to reservations west of the Mississippi River. The people were rounded up by United States Army troopers, herded together, and forced to march the long miles to the West. About 14,000 Cherokees started out on the 800-mile journey. Some 4,000 died along the way. The forced march through the bitter winter is known as "the trail of tears."

About 1,000 Cherokee people refused to be driven from their homeland. They ran deep into the mountains and forests, where they remained hidden for many years. While in hiding, they had a trader named Colonel William Holland Thomas buy land, which he kept in his own name because the Indians were forbidden by law to acquire property. The land was divided into six districts, three of which are named for Cherokee clans: Bird Town, Paint Town, and Wolf Town. The others are called Yellow Hill, Big Cove, and Snowbird. All the land, known as the Thomas Tract, is now part of the Cherokee Reservation in North Carolina.

Fifty years after the Cherokees' "trail of tears," those who had refused to leave North Carolina formally declared themselves a separate body from the Cherokee in the West. The eastern members organized themselves as the Eastern Band of the Cherokee, with their own elected council of twelve, a chief, and a vice chief. In 1925 the tribal council arranged with the United States government to hold title to the Cherokee land in trust for the people. The land on the reservation can be bought and sold among the Cherokee with the consent of the council. It can be leased to non-Indians for business purposes, but it is not for sale to them.

Community organizations have been formed among the Cherokee to help the people and to provide

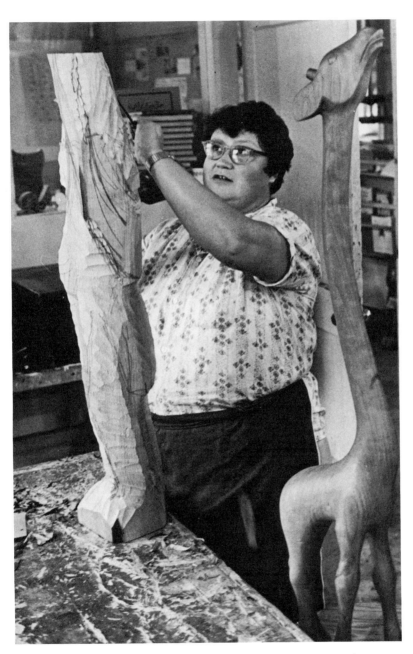

Amanda Crow, sculptor, with some of her animal figures, Cherokee,
North Carolina.

educational opportunities for the children. One of the major groups is the Cherokee Boys Farm Club, which operates a fleet of buses to transport Cherokee youngsters to elementary and high schools on the reservation. Facilities for preschool children and for adult education are also available. The reservation schools are financed by the federal government. Some Cherokee children attend off-reservation institutions, which are part of the state's school system.

Cherokee farmers no longer have extensive fields for their crops. Only the narrow plots along waterways or on the gentler lower slopes of the mountains can be used for cultivation. Much of the rest of the reservation is mountainous and impossible to till. The forests, however, can still be worked by woodsmen and lumbermen, who make wood products from the trees. Others of the tribe are employed in factories, located on the reservation, which produce textiles, leather goods, and cosmetics. The major sources of employment for the Cherokee, however, are the federal government agencies and the local businesses serving the many thousands of tourists who visit the Great Smoky Mountains every year.

Hotels, restaurants, and craft shops on the Cherokee reservation cater to the many visitors. Some of the tourists come to see the Indians, some to enjoy the natural scenery of the Great Smoky Mountains, and some to attend the theatrical pageants, which are staged during the summer to dramatize Cherokee history.

Both traditional and modern Cherokee arts and crafts are sold, mainly in the city of Cherokee. Adept woodcarvers fashion traditional Iroquois false face masks, as well as wooden figures and other decorative objects. Cherokee women weave baskets, utilizing natural material from the forests: honeysuckle vines, wild hemp, river cane, and splints of white oak or ash. To

Wood carver Sim Jessan shapes a ceremonial mask, Cherokee
Reservation, North Carolina.

Margaret Wahneetah French, as a child, on doorstep of Cherokee Indian home in North Carolina mountains.

make the baskets colorful, they use dyes also derived from woodland sources, such as roots or the bark of oak, maple, or walnut trees.

Other Cherokee artists, preserving the skills of their ancestors, make beaded belts, headbands, and decorated moccasins and coats. The Indians did not use glass beads until they were introduced to them by the European settlers. Earlier Indians used shell, bone, animal teeth, stones, and feathers to decorate their clothing and to make ornaments.

Because they had become organized corn farmers, the Cherokee also became accomplished potters, a skill that stems from the need to store and prepare grain and seed. The Cherokee made well-fashioned bowls, jars, pots, and pipes from native clays. Like all the Indians of

Eva Wolfe, basketweaver, with some of her work, Cherokee, North Carolina.

the Americas, the Cherokee were unfamiliar with the true potter's wheel, used to shape a clay vessel. They used instead the coiling method, which consisted of building up the walls of the pot by piling strips or ropes of clay on top of one another. The walls were smoothed with a wooden paddle and then polished with a stone before being baked in outdoor ovens.

Some Cherokee pottery was for everyday use, and some for ceremonial use. At one time the Cherokee celebrated six festivals every year: the First New Moon of Spring Festival in March, the Green Corn Ceremony in August, the Ripe Corn Festival in early fall, the Bouncing Bush Feast in September, the Great New Moon Ceremony in October, and the Friendship Ceremony in October or November. Every seventh year they performed the Uku, or Chief Dance.

Some of the older Cherokee people still remember the ceremonial dances, some of which are performed by large groups, moving slowly in a circle to the music of flutes, drums, and gourd or turtle-shell rattles. One of the best known Cherokee dances is the Eagle Dance, in which the dancers wave wands of eagle feathers as they perform. The eagle wand is a symbol of peace for the Cherokee, who regard the bird and its feathers as sacred objects. Other natural creatures and objects, such as the rattlesnake, fire, smoke, the sun, the moon, and corn, are also held in reverence by the Cherokee.

In addition to the approximately 5,000 members of the Eastern Band of the Cherokee who live on the reservation in the Great Smoky Mountains, there are many others who live away from the reserve.

Descendants of the Cherokee people who went west during the early 1800s are still in Oklahoma. Their estimated population is over 50,000.

Another group of Indians, the Waccamaw, also live in North Carolina. Their population is listed as about 2,000. Most of the Waccamaw are located in the southeastern corner of the state, near the lake and river that bear their tribal name.

The meaning of the name is unknown. Nothing of the tribe's original language has been preserved, but it is thought to have been connected with the Siouan language family. The Sioux Indians were primarily western tribes, whose name is the abbreviation of an Indian word meaning "adders" or "enemies." Their name for themselves was *Dakota* or *Lakota*, meaning "allies." Probably the Waccamaw were related to the Siouan-speaking Catawba Indians of South Carolina.

The Waccamaw enjoy no special government services and do not live on reservation land.

SOUTH CAROLINA

More than 2,200 people in South Carolina listed themselves as Indians in the 1970 census. This is approximately twice as many as were recorded in 1960 and 1930. In 1900 the official Indian population for the state was only 121.

Of South Carolina's 2,241 Indian residents, less than 400 are members of the state's last official tribe— the Catawba. The others include a scattering of Waccamaw Indians, whose main tribal grouping is in North Carolina, and small groups of people identified as social isolates. These people have no proven Indian history, and their identity as Indians is not certain. However, they may have descended from remnants of ancient groups of Catawba Indians, who inhabited the Piedmont Mountains, and Algonquian tribes, who once lived along the coastal plains. The largest social isolate group in South Carolina today is called the Brass Ankles, for reasons unknown. Another group of about 250, called the Summerville Indians, lives in Dorchester and Colleton counties.

CATAWBA
origin unknown

When the Catawba Indians were first encountered by Europeans, the tribe probably numbered over 5,000. Through the years, however, the Catawba have been devastated by warfare and smallpox. The current tribal group probably includes the remnants of twenty related tribes, who once lived nearby.

During the colonial period the Catawba, a Siouan-speaking people, allied themselves with the English against the Iroquois-speakers, the Cherokee and the Tuscarora. At the end of the American Revolution the Catawba had years of comparative prosperity, acting as intermediaries and traders between the Carolinas and Virginia.

In 1763 the tribe was settled on a reservation fifteen miles square in York and Lancaster counties, near South Carolina's northern border. By 1841 the reservation land had dwindled to about one square mile. About 60 Catawba still live on the reservation site, near the city of Rock Hill.

For about a century after 1841 the tribe eked out a poor existence on the reservation by fishing, berry

Three Catawba Indian youngsters in South Carolina in 1913.

picking, woodcutting, and selling pottery, which they still produce in an ancient and traditional style. Then in 1943 the Catawba Indians, the state of South Carolina, and the federal government joined forces to form a "new" reservation. Tax-exempt lands were bought and a program was begun to rehabilitate the people. Catawba children were enrolled in the public schools, and the United States government provided some aid for education, health, and welfare. A track of 3,388 acres was established on which 631 Catawba resided.

The new reservation land was divided among eighty-eight individual Indians, to be used for home building and farming. One portion of the land was set aside as a timber stand and a cattle range. The tribe as a whole reserved the water, mineral, and timber rights.

In 1961–62, however, the federal government ended its relationship with the Catawba, no longer providing any special services for them. The tribally owned land was divided among the individual Catawba, who also received a share of the proceeds from the sale of the tribe's beef herd.

The Catawba are the only Eastern Indians whose religious beliefs are patterned after the Mormons of Utah.

GEORGIA

Georgia no longer has any major tribal groups, although 2,347 state residents were listed as Indians in the 1970 census. This was a threefold increase since 1960 and a huge leap since 1930 and 1900, when the state's Indian population was forty-three and nineteen, respectively.

In colonial times and earlier, Georgia was the home of great numbers of Indians belonging to the Creek Confederacy, a loose organization of tribes spread over both Georgia and Alabama. The Confederacy centered around a group of powerful tribes called the Muskogee, whose name came to be applied to the entire language family of many southeastern tribes. Other tribes in the Creek Confederacy were the Guale, the

CREEK
derived from Ocheese Creek,
now Ocmulgee River

Yamasee, the Yuchi, and probably even some Algonquian-speaking Shawnee. Many Cherokee Indians also lived in Georgia before being forced to move to the West.

Creek Indian of late 18th century.

Chief of Creek Indian nation and his nephew, from an engraving after an early 18th century portrait.

Neither the Creek nor the Cherokee form distinct tribal groupings in Georgia. However, several hundred people claiming Cherokee heritage live along the northern border of the state, and a small settlement of Indians still exists in Burke County, ten miles south of the city of Augusta. Also in the state is a group of 100 or fewer Croatan, or Altamaha, Indians, remnants of Siouan-speaking tribes.

Georgia Indians receive no special services from the state. They occupy no reservations and no longer speak any Indian language.

FLORIDA

Nearly 7,000 Indians reside in Florida. The 1970 census figure of 6,677 is more than twice the 1960 figure and is far greater than the 587 and 358 Indians listed in the state in 1930 and 1900, respectively.

The primary tribespeople of Florida are known as Seminoles, a name probably meaning "the ones who camped out of the regular towns." Sometimes the name has been translated as "fugitives" or "runaways." Its meaning is better expressed as "wild"—as a deer is wild and free.

Florida Indians are members of the fourth major Indian language group along the Atlantic seaboard—the Muskogean language family. Within this family, how-

██

SEMINOLE
"the wild ones" or
"fugitives" or "runaways"

██

ever, the Seminole are divided into two distinct linguistic groups. The Seminole tongues of both groups are still spoken.

The larger group, numbering about 1,600, is called the Muskogee, or Cow Creek Seminole. They are also known as the Reservation Indians, or officially, the Seminole Tribe of Florida. Their language is derived from the Creek Indian tongue spoken by their ancestors in Georgia several hundred years ago. The meaning of the name *Muskogee* is not definitely known, but it may be from a Western Indian language, the Shawnee, and refer to swampy ground.

The smaller group, with a membership of approximately 500, is known as the Miccosukee Tribe of Indians, or Trail Indians. Their variation of the Muskogean language is known as Hitchiti. The meaning of the name is unknown.

██

APALACHICOLA
"the people of the other side"

██

The remainder of Florida's Indians are unaffiliated with the two organized tribes and are either living in isolated communities or in the larger cities, intermingled with the general population. One group is called the Apalachicola, "the people of the other side," referring probably to the river of that name.

The Seminole have not always lived in Florida. At one time they lived in Georgia and Alabama, where they were members of the Creek Confederacy. They moved southward early in the 1700s, when many of the original Indians of Florida were captured by Spanish explorers and traders and sold into slavery, leaving behind unoccupied lands. The Seminole ancestors were attracted to these empty areas and moved into them, making northern Florida their homeland.

Spanish control in Florida lasted for many years after the thirteen colonies had become states. Because the area was outside the boundaries of the United States, it seemed a place of safety for slaves running away from southern plantations. The slaves found shelter with the Seminole. However, when the plantation owners came searching for the escaped slaves, they often destroyed the Indians' crops and homes.

In 1818 General Andrew Jackson led an American army into Spanish-held Florida. His action led to the First Seminole War.

In 1821 Spain, unable to control the Florida territory, ceded it to the United States. Immediately a campaign was launched to make the Seminole leave their homes and settle in the West. This led to the Second Seminole War in 1835. The Indians fought bitterly against the American armies, but many were taken captive and shipped west. The war ended in 1842, when the remaining Seminole fled into the wilderness of the Everglades, where they established a new way of life, far from the pressures of American society.

The Third Seminole War broke out in 1855 and lasted for three years. American troops pursued the elusive Indians into the Everglades swamplands, destroying their villages and crops. However, only 123 Seminole were rounded up and moved west. The rest of the tribe faded even deeper into the swamps and stayed out of sight.

More than eighty years later, in 1938, the Third Seminole War officially came to an end. A truce was signed between the Seminole and the United States, but a treaty of peace has never been made. The reason is a federal law that prohibits the United States from signing any treaties with Indian tribes within its own territory.

When the Seminole fled from northern Florida into the Everglades to avoid forced migration to the West, their way of life underwent many changes. Their homes, clothing, and arts and crafts all had to be adapted to the subtropical climate and swampy terrain of southern Florida.

From the log cabins they had once occupied, the Seminole turned to building chickees, light, open, airy shelters ideally suited to the hot, wet climate of the Everglades. There are two kinds of chickees; one is a shelter for sleeping, and the other is a cooking structure, traditionally shared by an entire community. Both are made of a framework of poles cut from small trees and covered by a roof of thatched palmetto fronds, overlapping downward. The roof is sharply angled to keep the dwelling dry from driving subtropical rainstorms; the roof edges drain well beyond the living area.

Chickees have no walls to exclude the cooling winds, which give welcome relief on hot, humid days and blow away bothersome insects. The lack of walls is also a safeguard, for without them there is no rigid structure to be blown down by hurricanes and other strong winds.

The sleeping chickee has a bed platform built about three feet above the ground. The low tablelike floor keeps the inhabitants safe from crawling insects and snakes. During the day the bedding is taken away and the platform beds become serving tables and workbenches. For many years a sewing machine has been a

Seminole elders, in traditional clothing, hew a canoe from a log.

part of nearly every Seminole household, and today many families have other manufactured articles, including television sets.

The cooking chickee usually is the center of a traditional Seminole encampment. It is a floorless structure with a palmetto roof. Large logs are spread out on the ground of the chickee like the spokes of a wheel. Over the burning coals in the center a pot of thin gruel, called sofkee, hangs bubbling almost all of the time.

In the Everglades National Park modern chickees have been developed. Large and well-ventilated, they are made of concrete or wood and have electric lights and cooking ranges, hot water, and complete bathrooms. The roofs, however, are still thatched with palm fronds.

Some Seminole Indians, of course, live in regular modern houses in communities that seem like any other community. But many still prefer the traditional chickee and the small isolated encampment of their ancestors.

When they moved into the Everglades, the Seminole changed their clothing from buckskin and leather to cotton shirts and skirts, which were much cooler. Over the years Seminole tribal dress has become very colorful. Much of their clothing is made from many bands of bright-colored, bold-patterned cloth, sewn together on the ever-present sewing machine.

Seminole men usually wear a vividly colored knee-length shirt or blouse, made with geometric designs—lines, squares, and rectangles. Even for everyday dress they tie a bright scarf around their throats.

Seminole women wear skirts sewn from bands of bright-colored cloth for tribal dress. Their blouses are usually white, with capelike sleeves and bands of colored cloth on the collar and cuffs. They also wear strings upon strings of bright beads, which they begin collect-

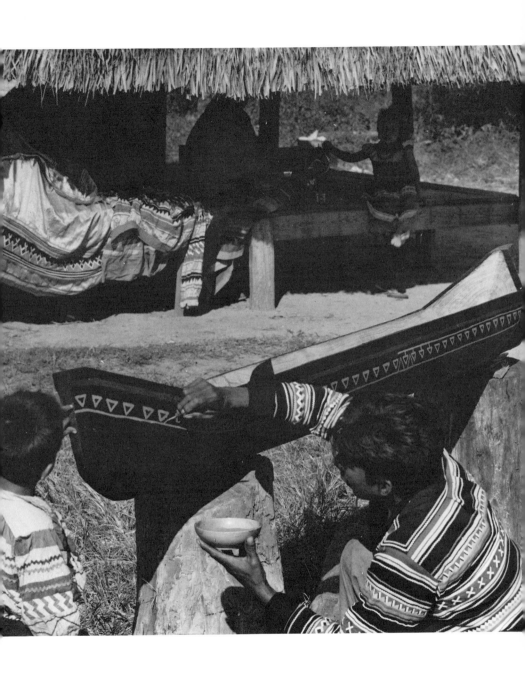

Seminole boys paint wooden canoe. Traditional open chickee in background.

ing in childhood, receiving their first string at birth. On their heads Seminole women often wear a large hairpiece called a rat, which makes their hair stand up high in a comblike style.

How this unique Seminole dress developed is not certain. Some people think it is a copy of old non-Indian styles. Others believe it was inspired by the colorfully banded tree snails that live in the Everglades. Still others think that it grew out of the scarcity of cloth among the early Seminoles. At that time every scrap of cloth was guarded with care, and when enough bits of material were gathered, they were made into a garment.

Sewing bright-colored clothing for tribal use and for sale is one of the characteristic crafts of the Seminole. Tribal artists are also talented basketmakers, beadwork weavers, and woodcarvers. In times past the people became experts at making dugout canoes from cypress trees in order to navigate the wetlands of the Everglades. While still in northern Florida, the Seminole were also skilled weavers, leatherworkers, and potters. But these arts were difficult to pursue in the swamplands. Today tribespeople are working to revive some of the ancient arts, particularly the production of native earthenware.

Over the years several federal reservations and one state reserve have been established in Florida. Approximately 400 members of the Seminole Tribe of Florida occupy the Hollywood Reservation, which was once known as the Dania Reserve. It covers 475 acres west of the city of Fort Lauderdale. More than 320 Seminole Tribe members have homes on the Brighton Reservation, which occupies 35,795 acres on the west side of Lake Okeechobee, and about 340 live on the Big Cypress Reservation, spread over 42,698 acres in the midst of the Everglades.

Community cooking fire, attended by Seminole woman and girls,
Okalee Village.

The Miccosukee Tribe has a 323-acre reservation
along the northern edges of the Everglades National
Park. Approximately 430 people live there.

The Florida State Reservation, which has no official
name yet, is located alongside the Big Cypress Reserve.
It is an area of 106,240 acres, without a single inhabi-
tant.

The Seminole Tribe of Florida was the first officially organized Indian group in the state. It was formed by
agreement with the federal government in 1957. The
tribe is headed by an elected tribal council of eight

Seminole cattlemen brand calf in tribe's stockyards.

members, which deals with government, education, welfare, recreation, and other tribal affairs.

Many of the Seminole people are employed in businesses that serve the thousands of tourists who visit the Florida Everglades. Tribe members conduct a number of tourist attractions, one of the most important being the Seminole Okalee Indian Village, twenty miles north of Miami. In the village is an Arts and Crafts Center, where Indian handicrafts are sold.

Cattle raising has become an important occupation for the Seminole on the Brighton and Big Cypress reservations. Once the herd was owned by the tribe as a whole, but in 1953 the cattle were sold to individual

Seminole Indian cowboys on horseback at roundup time.

Indians who are cowboys and ranchers. The cattle graze on large-scale artificially irrigated pasturage. Seminole cattlemen wear typical western-style hats, trousers, and shirts.

Members of the Seminole Tribe also work as harvesters on local truck farms and hold jobs in nearby lumber camps. Some have become skillful mechanics and expert handlers of the heavy machinery used in construction work.

Other employment opportunities for the Seminole may be opening on their reserves in the future. A factory to build house trailers is being planned for the Brighton Reservation. There are also plans for a recreation center, which would include a marina on Lake Okeechobee. At Big Cypress Reservation roads will open sand and gravel resources and will make camping and hunting grounds easily accessible.

The education of Seminole Tribe children is generally handled on the reservations during the early grades and off the reservations during later grades. For example, on the Big Cypress Reservation a day school is maintained from kindergarten through fourth grade. From the fifth grade through high school, the children travel by bus to off-reservation schools in a city almost fifty miles away.

The Miccosukee Tribe of Indians was officially organized and recognized by the United States government in June 1962. Its constitution specifically prohibits outside efforts to change tribal customs and religious beliefs. The Miccosukee hope to protect their traditional culture and to make only voluntary changes in their living habits.

Besides the approximately 430 members of the official tribe on the reservation, there are several hundred Miccosukee Seminole living close by in the swamps and lowlands along the Tamiami Trail. The Trail is a highway that extends approximately 100 miles across the state, connecting Miami and the Gulf Coast city of Naples.

A general council is the governing body of the Miccosukee Tribe. Its officers are a chairman, assistant chairman, secretary, treasurer, and a lawmaker, who also acts as the tribe's business officer. The general council deals with matters of government, law, order, education, welfare, recreation, and finances. The business officer is charged with the day-to-day commercial affairs of the tribe.

Jurisdiction in all civil and criminal matters is

Seminole couple in a log canoe, drifting through Everglades.

maintained over the Indians by the counties and the
state of Florida.

The building of highways through the Everglades
opened up many remote Indian areas, and the coming
of non-Indians brought problems to the Miccosukee
people. Many of their traditional ways of life, particularly their occupations as hunters and fishermen, had to
change. Nevertheless, from November to March each
year, the men of the tribe go into the swamps and hunt
frogs, which sell readily in the food markets of Miami.
Some Miccosukee have found new work on local vege-
table farms and as part-time laborers.

Many tribespeople are employed in modern businesses established by the tribe itself. In 1964 the Miccosukee Tribe built a large, attractive restaurant approximately forty miles west of Miami along the Tamiami Trail. Near it they built a service station for passing motorists and a grocery store. A Miccosukee village is also located on the Tamiami Trail and has become a well-known tourist attraction.

Before the Miccosukee Tribe was officially organized, the Indian children did not attend school. Late in 1962 a one-room portable schoolhouse was made available for nineteen students of the first class. The teacher was supplied by the Bureau of Indian Affairs. A year later a second teacher was required to handle the increased enrollment. Two years later a modern building was put up, with two classrooms, a kitchen, and a cafeteria. A gymnasium was provided in a community building.

The Miccosukee children study in their own school until the fourth or fifth grade, primarily because of a language barrier. The children's mother tongue is still the ancient Indian Hitchiti language of their ancestors, and they must learn English before they can attend schools off the reservation.

In addition to elementary education for Miccosukee children, the adult members of the tribe are provided with studies in nutrition, health, community affairs, finance, safety, and other subjects.

Although modern society has penetrated their lives, the Indians of Florida still have a strong group identity, which they proudly and courageously uphold. Many still adhere to their traditional religious beliefs and try to live according to their ancient culture. For the Seminole, as for many Indians of the Atlantic seaboard, the old ways persist, even while the people prepare to live in modern times.

CENSUS OF EASTERN INDIANS
OF THE UNITED STATES
(According to the 1970 Census)

	1970	1960	1930	1900
NEW ENGLAND DIVISION				
Maine............	2,195	1,879	1,012	798
New Hampshire..	361	135	64	22
Vermont.........	229	57	36	5
Massachusetts	4,475	2,118	874	587
Rhode Island.....	1,390	932	318	35
Connecticut......	2,222	923	162	153
	10,872	6,044	2,466	1,600
MIDDLE ATLANTIC DIVISION				
New York........	28,355	16,491	6,973	5,257
New Jersey.......	4,706	1,699	213	63
Pennsylvania......	5,533	2,122	523	1,639
	38,594	20,312	7,709	6,959
SOUTH ATLANTIC DIVISION				
Delaware.........	656	597	5	9
Maryland.........	4,239	1,538	50	3
District of Columbia....	956	587	40	22
Virginia..........	4,853	2,155	779	354
North Carolina...	44,406	38,129	16,579	5,687
South Carolina....	2,241	1,098	959	121
Georgia..........	2,347	749	43	19
Florida..........	6,677	2,504	587	358
	66,375	47,357	19,042	6,573
Total............	115,841	73,713	29,217	15,132

BIBLIOGRAPHY

Up-to-date material about the Eastern Indians of the United States is not easily available. A great deal has been written about the early historical periods, covering the eras of discovery and colonization. Literature about more recent periods, however, seems to have dwindled away, as though supporting the idea that the people themselves have vanished. This situation is changing.

FOR YOUNGER READERS

Brandon, William. *American Indians,* American Heritage Book of Indians edited for younger readers. New York: Random House, 1963.

Glubok, Shirley. *The Art of the North American Indians.* New York: Harper and Row, 1964.

LaFarge, Oliver. *A Pictorial History of the American Indian.* New York: Crown, 1956.

———. *The American Indian.* New York: Western, 1960.

Stirling, Matthew, ed. *Indians of America.* Washington, D.C.: National Geographic Society, 5th printing.

Tunis, Edwin. *Indians.* Cleveland: World, 1959.

FOR THE GENERAL READER BY NON-INDIAN AUTHORS

Bureau of Indian Affairs. *The Indians of the Eastern Seaboard. The Indians of North Carolina. The Indians of the Gulf Coast States. Indians and Eskimo Children.* Washington, D.C.: U.S. Government Printing Office.

Census Bureau. *American Indians.* Washington, D.C.: U.S. Government Printing Office, 1970.

Collier, John. *Indians of the Americas.* New York: Norton, 1947.

Driver, Harold E. *Indians of North America,* 2nd ed., rev. Chicago: University of Chicago Press, 1969.

Feder, Norman. *Two-hundred Years of North American Indian Art.* New York: Praeger, 1971.

Indian Arts and Crafts Board, Department of the Interior. *Native American Arts,* nos. 1 and 2. Washington, D.C.: U.S. Government Printing Office.

Interdepartmental Committee on Indian Affairs, New York State. *The Indian Today in New York State,* annual. Albany, New York: Interdepartmental Committee on Indian Affairs.

Josephy, Alvin M., Jr., ed. *The American Heritage Book of Indians.* New York: American Heritage, 1961.

————. *The Indian Heritage of America.* New York: Knopf and Bantam, 1968.

Ritchie, William A. *Indian History of New York State.* Albany, New York: State Museum and Science Service, 1953.

Sturtevant, William C., and Stanley, Samuel. *Indian Communities in the Eastern States.* San Francisco: *Indian Historian,* Vol. 1, No. 3, 1968.

Swanton, John R. *The Indians of the Southeastern United States.* Washington, D.C.: Bureau of American Ethnology, Bulletin 137, 1946.

————. *The Indian Tribes of North America.* Washington, D.C.: Bureau of Ethnology, Bulletin 145, 1968.

Taylor, Theodore W. *The States and Their Indian Citizens.* Washington, D.C.: Bureau of Indian Affairs, Department of the Interior, 1972.

FOR THE GENERAL READER BY INDIAN AUTHORS

Costo, Rupert, ed., and Henry, Jeannette, author. *Textbooks and the American Indian.* San Francisco: Indian Historical Press, 1970.

DeLoria, Vinnie. *Custer Died for Your Sins.* Toronto: Macmillan, 1969.

Momaday, N. Scott. *House Made of Dawn.* New York: Harper and Row, 1968.

Aren, Akweks. *Migration of the Tuscarora. Four Happenings in Indian History.* Onchiota, New York: Six Nations Indian Museum.

Nicholas, Barry, dir. *Report on the Indian Education Workshop.* Bar Harbor, Maine: T.R.I.B.E.

INDIAN NEWSPAPERS AND MAGAZINES

Akwesasne Notes (newspaper). Roosevelttown, New York.

Cherokee One-Feather (newspaper). Cherokee, North Carolina.

Indian Historian (magazine). Issued by the American Indian Historical Society, San Francisco.

Tsen Akamak (newspaper). Powhatan, Virginia.

Wassaja (newspaper). Issued by the American Indian Historical Society, San Francisco.

Weewish Tree, The (magazine for children). Issued by the American Indian Historical Society, San Francisco.

INDEX